SEA of GLORY

SEA of GLORY

THE MAGNIFICENT STORY OF THE
FOUR CHAPLAINS

Francis Beauchesne Thornton

PRENTICE-HALL, INC.
NEW YORK

To
All Men
Who Have Died
For Their Country

ACKNOWLEDGMENTS

This book is a practical demonstration of inter-faith co-operation and love. People of all races and creeds helped me with it. They made the labor of collecting the material a heart-warming experience.

I am deeply grateful to the following organizations and individuals who helped in assembling and checking the facts in this book: The Department of the Army—Maj. Gen. Edward F. Witsell, Maj. Gen. William E. Bergin, Maj. Gen. K. B. Bush. Personal Information Bureau—Col. T. J. Marnane. Chaplains' Corps—Col. William J. Reiss, Col. Matthew H. Imrie, Col. Patrick J. Ryan, Col. Charles E. Brown. Methodist Commission of Chaplains; National Jewish Welfare Board—Rabbi Aryeh Lev, Rabbi David Max Eichhorn; Congressman John F. Shelly. Most Rev. William R. Arnold; Jewish Community Center, York, Pa.— J. Sperling.

Also to Dr. Daniel A. Poling, Bishop G. Bromley Oxnam, Dr. Arthur Workman, Rev. Bertram De Heus Atwood, Rabbi Hyman S. Goode, Rabbi Eli Pilchik, Rt. Rev. Thomas Powers, Rt. Rev. Justin McCarthy, Rev. Denis Whalen, Rev. James Cunningham, Rev. Frank McCue, Rev. Gordon Byrne, Rev. Joseph Curtin, Rev. Richard D. Wall, Rev. Donald J. Wagner, Rev. Christopher Murphy, Rev. John Flanneily, Rev. Joseph D. O'Leary.

ACKNOWLEDGMENTS

Also to Mrs. Frank Washington, Mr. and Mrs. L. Schwoebel, Mr. and Mrs. Alvin Schroth, Theresa Goode, Joseph Goode, Nathan Brown, Carrie Simons, Dr. Victoria Lyles, Jason B. Snyder, Dr. James O'Connell, Leo Washington, Betty Gayle Fitzsimmons, Mr. and Mrs. George Painter, Dr. William J. Reagan, Dr. and Mrs. Curtis Newlin, Dr. John Pick, Dr. and Mrs. P. S. Healy, Mrs. Mary De Matteis, L. W. Green, C. C. "Doc" Bleeker, Adolph Kuntz, Freda Egbert, Margaret Judge, Agnes Curran, Mrs. Joseph Duffy, Mrs. Isabelle Eaton Davis, Floyd Reinecker, Jacob Weber, Tom Peoples, Mr. and Mrs. John P. Wilde, Patrick Gantley, Theodore Granik, Mr. and Mrs. Paul L. Taylor, Mrs. George Marsh, Archibald Wemple, Douw F. Beekman, Mrs. Amos R. Wells, Mr. and Mrs. John Edmands, Mrs. Malcolm Hill, Mr. and Mrs. W. D. Hanbridge, Mrs. Mary McCormack, James Friday, Alta McKague, Raymond Shank, John Barnhart, Ruby Jackson, Edith Kuhn, Gertrude Unverdorben, Hayes Lynam, Mrs. George Fowlie, Mrs. Myles Quigley, Mrs. Mabel Woodbury, Mrs. Leslie Briggs, Mrs. Claude Briggs, Mrs. O. E. Randall, Mrs. Marjorie Rainney, Eunice Harvey, Martha Lobeck, Dr. James R. Joy, M. Dorothy Woodruff, Rev. Daniel Poling, Jr., Dr. and Mrs. Alexander B. Sinclair, Jr., Rev. Paul Bussard, Timothy Murphy Rowe, and to Commander Allan Keller, U.S.N.R.

FRANCIS BEAUCHESNE THORNTON

SEA of GLORY

~~~~~~~~~~~~~~~~~~~~~~~~~~~~The freighter rose and fell sluggishly at her pier, her spring lines alternately slack and tight. In the darkness beneath the flooring, down at the water line of the rusty ship, there was the slap of the waves against her sides and against the pilings—one of the loneliest sounds that can haunt man's ears.

Floodlamps turned the New England night into a garish noon, a noon full of shadows, and full of the sound of winches, of screeching cranes and booms and of the shuffling cadence of weary troops, keeping step out of habit rather than from conscious desire.

One of the shadows the lights didn't reach hung near the stern of the freighter, almost obliterating her name—the *Dorchester*— but neither the glare of the light nor the kindness of the shadows could hide the fact that the vessel was old, and small, and probably slow—or that she would undoubtedly pitch and roll even in good weather, and would yaw crazily in heavy seas.

Soldiers climbing the gangplank looked at the *Dorchester* as though they had been cheated in a poker game even before the cards were dealt. One whose humor had not been erased by hours of standing and marching spoke over his shoulder to another man behind him.

"She'd fit in a funnel of the *Queen Mary*. She's no bigger than a lifeboat."

He was right. She was devoid of class. Whatever dignity she was to possess would have to go aboard her in the hearts and breasts of the soldiers using her as a ferry to the bloody fields of war. She had none of her own.

She was listed with Lloyds' at 5000 tons and the symbols in the Register, when translated, meant that she was just another workhorse of the sea, intended to carry slow cargo in her holds. Only the exigencies of total war had forced her transformation into a troopship.

On this night in January, 1943, she was being loaded with troops at a Massachusetts port, her destination hidden in an envelope of secret orders, the seal of which would stay unbroken until she had lumbered into position in a convoy, hours out of sight of land.

Deckhands, fighting the winter cold in reefers close-collared against the wind, moved about her decks with the slow precision of veteran seamen. Lights atop the king posts and the bridge illuminated the open hatches through which was being lowered the gear and apparatus of war. The booms, swinging from ship to pier and back again, complained with the strident sound of steel rasping against steel.

The tide was running out and the freighter chafed at her moorings, moving in a short arc within the confines of her hawsers. The motion caused the gangplank to move back and forth too, the lower end, supported by small wheels, rolling unevenly on the floorboards of the pier.

Each enlisted man, his duffel bag on his shoulder, had to break step as he reached the gangplank. Sometimes a foot would be poised for the first step and then the plank would pull away like a hoydenish thing. Again it would move drunkenly the other way, forcing the soldier to quickstep to protect himself.

Historians could speak of this contrivance in later years as a bridge to man's victory against the forces of totalitarian evil. It was a narrow, unstable link between the known and the unknown, between the safety of the shore and home and the awful dangers of the sea. Each man, tired and cold as he was that January night, must have thought about it as he plodded up the incline and stepped upon the steel plates of the freighter's deck.

There were humble GIs and equally humble officers who made the crossing from the pier to the *Dorchester*. A nameless fear quickened the pulse of every one of them, whether they spoke of it or not.

Among their number, carrying duffel bags like the rest, but

[5]

without the reassuring strength that comes from rifle or side-arms, walked four chaplains. Their names—Fox, Goode, Poling and Washington—told nothing.

On that night in January, 1943, destiny was curtained off completely. One by one, the army chaplains judged the eccentric behavior of the plank, adjusted their strides to match it, and stepped aboard the freighter, never dreaming the contraption was also a gangplank to everlasting glory.

Fox was a Methodist, called to duty from a snowbound parish in Vermont. Poling, another Protestant, had quit a comfortable existence in upstate New York. Goode, a Jewish Rabbi born in Brooklyn, was fresh from a synagogue in rural Pennsylvania. Washington, the man with the odd name, was a Catholic priest born and bred in industrial New Jersey.

They shared a cabin on the *Dorchester*—a cabin in name only, not much different from the sleeping quarters of the enlisted men—dreary, airless and heavy with the stench of fuel oil and bilge slop.

Fox was one up on his companions. He had gone overseas in the first World War—that time as a fighting man—and he knew the dirty business at its worst.

"I've been through this before," he said, stowing away his belongings to save space in the cramped room. "But with all these green kids and civilian workers it won't be any picnic. We'll make it all right, though."

Young Poling let the words hang suspended in the stuffy air, as they hung in each man's mind, while his stomach adjusted itself to the ship's motion.

"I'm a pretty good sailor," he said finally, "but when I crossed before I wasn't responsible for anyone but myself."

Soldiers tramped through the companionway outside, down

into the bowels of the *Dorchester*. Naked light bulbs showed them their quarters—bunks hastily built into the holds, four tiers high, six niggardly feet of space per man—just enough room for a night's sleep, or for that last, long sleep from which there is no awakening.

The scrape of hobnails on steel decks, the creaking of the booms and the whole mad cacophony of sound that grew out of the process of packing hundreds of men into narrow confines almost drowned out Father Washington's words.

"At least you've been to sea," he laughed. "I can't swim well enough to paddle across a duck pond. How about you, Alex?"

Rabbi Goode thrust his hands out. The other chaplains saw that his fingers were crossed and they guffawed.

"The way I see it," said Goode, "is this. We'll be so doggone busy with the men we won't have time to think of ourselves. Let's go topside for a minute. Maybe we aren't handsome, but if they catch us there smiling as they come aboard maybe it will kid them along a bit."

So they went up, making wrong turns in the narrow passageways as landlubbers always do, emerging on the starboard side aft when they had expected to come out forward on the port side. They laughed at their mistake and crossed to watch the dogfaces coming aboard like ants toiling to the top of their hill to disappear suddenly at the summit.

The men's faces were bleak, as only fighting men's faces can be, shoving off for overseas, or moving out on a patrol when the high brass, warm and safe at the rear, sends up orders to bring in prisoners for questioning or to apply more pressure in a diversion to protect the next division on one's flank.

It's the eyes that tell the story. The healthy glint that is any man's birthright grows lack-lustre on the eve of battle or danger.

The sockets become a little deeper, stretching the skin into shadowed crowsfeet. So it was with these men coming aboard the *Dorchester*. They could only guess at the future.

The port of embarkation camp had been one vast rumor factory. They were going to Africa. They were going to Northern Ireland. They were part of a secret movement destined for a landing up some Norwegian fjord. There was a vital plant to be destroyed—something about heavy water—it didn't make any sense but they were going to pull the Limey's chestnuts out of the fire again.

On board the *Dorchester* it was worse. Scuttlebutt passed from mouth to ear and on again with the speed of light. It was Africa. No it wasn't. It was Greenland. The Nazis had executed their promised invasion of England and they'd all be thrown into the fighting somewhere in Cornwall the minute they hit land.

The sky pilots knew they were bound for Greenland . . . the godforsaken, ice-covered, glacier-tortured end of the world.

As preachers of the Word and as ministers to the sick of heart and body, the chaplains knew what life in a hurriedly thrown together outpost on the Greenland coast could be. Worse than the front. There would be bitter cold, nights and days when the sun could be only a memory, far below the horizon, and there would be the monotony and the boredom and the bitterness and the grousing and the endlessness of time unsweetened by the music of a woman's voice.

Fox and Poling and Goode knew this better than the priest, since each had left a wife behind, but Father Washington understood well enough the heavy duty that lay on all four if they were to make life a little more bearable for the youngsters coming over the side, being herded by top-kicks and ship's officers into the fetid compartments below.

Somehow the men were squared away. Their bags and gear were stacked from deck to deck, almost from bulkhead to bulkhead. Tin helmets hung from every projection or were suspended by their straps from the bunks. They swung and rocked with every movement of the ship, and if a man watched them long enough he came to know the overpowering grip of nausea.

Over the ship's loudspeakers came word that when the *Dorchester* put out to sea the soldiers were to wear or carry their life jackets with them day and night. Men looked at one another in silent dread, and their hands reached out to feel the strange garments; fat, puffy and silly with their little red lights on the back.

At 0600 the next morning the *Dorchester* cast off her lines and headed out to sea. She was slow-footed and moved awkwardly from swell to swell, giving her helmsman fits trying to compensate for both the bitter wind and her slowness to the rudder.

She had a way of sliding from a crest into the trough of the next wave as though hopelessly tired, and even in moderate seas she took too much green water over her bow. Her superstructure became coated with ice and her encrusted lines slapped loudly against the booms and king posts.

At Point Option—the preselected rendezvous off the Massachusetts coast—the *Dorchester* found herself the seventh and last ship of a small convoy. If she had had two or three more knots in her she might have been the Lucky Seventh. As she didn't, she was placed smack in the middle of the convoy, much to the shame of her crew and the joy of her troops.

In January of 1943 the North Atlantic was perhaps the bitterest battleground of all the fronts. Allied shipping, under constant attack by wolfpacks of Nazi U-boats, was being sunk almost as fast as it could be built. Men-of-war and planes to combat the submarines were still in perilously short supply.

The newest destroyers went with the fleet to guard the carriers and battlewagons pounding Japanese islands in the far Pacific. The bulk of those that were left stood guard with the fast convoys to the United Kingdom or formed the screens for baby aircraft carriers to constitute the killer groups that played such a large part in the ultimate defeat of the U-boats.

For such as the lumbering *Dorchester* and her sisters there were only a few Coast Guard cutters, refitted yachts and other make-do craft.

The GIs, watching the *Dorchester* take station that first morning out, saw that three Coast Guard cutters were their only escort.

On board the freighter the naval gun crew, commanded by Lieutenant William H. Arpaia, but recently a Chicago lawyer, sensed their responsibility and stood to their weapon day and night. The same thing was happening on hundreds of other ships that same hour, and the fact that it was almost a pitiful gesture of defiance against underwater marauders that could go faster submerged than the old rust-buckets themselves could do didn't change the situation a whit. Young kids barely out of indoctrination or boot schools polished their guns, drilled with dummy ammunition and watched the whole wide arc of the horizon for the feather of a periscope's wake, or the bubbling trail of a torpedo.

The *Dorchester* slugged it out against high winds and heavy waves. More than half of the troops aboard her were desperately seasick. With hatches dogged down, portholes closed and no air conditioning the holds became fetid with heat and bad air. Always there was the stink from the bilges, and to it was added the greasy smells from the galleys, the odor of men's sweat and the poisonous stench of vomit.

One soldier relieved himself, turned to a companion equally sick in the next bunk, and groaned.

"I love my wife and I know she loves me," he muttered. "But if she ever expects to see me again she'll have to make the crossing. Once I put my dogs down on dry land I'll never take them off."

Each day brought forth more morose scuttlebutt than the day before. One of the holds was filled with aviation gasoline. The *Dorchester* was only a floating coffin. Couldn't last two minutes if torpedoed. Someone in the crew had told someone among the troops that a workman, making hasty repairs for this very trip, had driven a nail straight through the hull into the water outside. It didn't matter that such stories were being told on every transport; they were believed by many of the seasick, fear-ridden men.

Even the stoutest-hearted worried about the rumor that somewhere on this very ship was a Nazi agent with a diabolical wireless set who was calling in a wolfpack of subs for a mass killing.

To men used to the wind-scorched prairies of Kansas, the peaceful hills of New England or the broad savannahs of the South the creaking of the *Dorchester's* steelwork as she "worked" in the pounding seas was a terrifying phenomenon.

Day became night and night became day again as the little convoy followed the course to Greenland, well off the headlands of Maine and the ominous, snow-scarfed coast of Canada.

Each morning the men were hustled above decks to go through lifeboat drill and they found themselves cursing the cold that numbed their fingers and frosted their faces. Most of them went below gladly, retreating to the warmth and its accompanying foul odors.

The days were bad enough, but the nights were empty voids of terror for many of the soldiers. Small lights in the holds, casting their eerie blue brightness, were no compensation for the blackness that enshrouded the whole convoy. Dangers that could be seen were bad enough. Those that couldn't were like icy fingers on a man's lungs. And always there was the pitching and the rolling and the crazy yawing of the freighter, and the endless creaking of the deck girders and the bulkheads.

There were some hardier men among them, some few accustomed to the sea and others gifted with a resilience they hadn't guessed at, who huddled in bull sessions, shot craps in the companionways and raided the crews' coffee mess. Some went to divine services and others didn't, but the four chaplains noticed that the farther the *Dorchester* beat her way from home the higher was the attendance.

The men noticed something too, as the days wore on. They couldn't help seeing that the four padres were all straight out of the top drawer. There wasn't a foul ball among them, one man said.

Chaplain Fox, the oldest, had been a fighting man. On his dress blouse he wore the ribbon of the Silver Star, awarded for gallantry somewhere between St. Mihiel and the Meuse-Argonne. He knew and understood men. He had been State Chaplain of the American Legion in Vermont for several years. He had groused at Army life when a boy himself. He knew how to dull the edge of that bitterness now that he was a minister.

Goode, Poling and Washington were younger, but as they moved about the men, passing out magazines, papers, and an occasional pill for seasickness, or bandying jokes and stories with the soldiers they showed they had an inner maturity that gave them strength.

Poling was a great one for a joke and his guffaws could be heard a long way as he went about his chores. He not only kidded the perpetual gripers among the soldiers but he kidded his fellow chaplains and the troops loved him for it.

Goode and Washington were a little more serious, perhaps, and a little quieter, but when a man was troubled and spiritually uneasy they were quick to say the word that gave support and fresh assurance.

If anyone had taken a poll, the vote among the GIs, sick, worried and disillusioned, would have proved their conviction that while the four chaplains—the two Protestants, the Catholic and the Jew—were men of God, they were first of all real men.

Their daily chores didn't leave much room for planning work in Greenland but when the four chaplains had a chance they talked about what they could do to make life more bearable at that barren outpost.

Father Washington, an outstanding athlete in high school and at the seminary, planned a broad sports program.

"You'll never have a game called on account of darkness in the summer," laughed Rabbi Goode. "The sun doesn't set for months."

Chaplain Poling teased Fox and Goode because they had gone to Chaplains' indoctrination school at Harvard.

"You got your training in the Ivy League," he said. "What a soft hitch. Washington and I didn't have it so easy."

The same sort of bantering was going on among the men. Maybe the language wasn't so discreet, but the idea behind it was the same. If they joked and kidded and laughed, maybe the steely fingers of fear would loosen a little about their hearts.

There was reason for the fear.

Word seeped down from the bridge and the radio shack that "Sparks," although never daring to send off a word, had heard many a dot-and-dash code message while listening to the endless chatter that even a war doesn't shut off.

There were lots of kraut subs around and they knew, it seemed, where the convoys were, and they must have been talking back and forth among themselves about a rendezvous at some not-too-distant "torpedo junction."

As the *Dorchester* and her companions zig-zagged along at their maddening pace, they saw that the Coast Guard cutters formed a pitifully thin screen. One usually went ahead, one stayed astern and the other circled or backed and filled wherever it seemed it could do the most good.

Twice they passed through patches still heavy with the reek of bunker oil, and once they saw the flotsam and jetsam of sudden death in the North Atlantic. A shattered lifeboat, an oil drum and empty life rafts floated by in a terrifying tableau of tragedy.

The soldiers on deck looked at the evidence of war's bitterness and found themselves swallowing with difficulty. The padres were there and saw it too. Because they were men first and chaplains second, they too knew the sudden clutch of terror.

A minister of God can coach himself to look upon Death with some modicum of faith and resignation. Goode, Fox, Washington and Poling had watched terror come to many a person's eyes as the sand in the hourglass trickled lower. They had spoken the words that must be spoken in many a saddened home and by many an open grave.

But here on the storm-tortured sea, a thousand miles from anywhere, they found that they too were thinking of loved ones at home, asking themselves questions for which they knew the answers far too well.

Increasingly they spoke to one another of childhood days, of family memories and of the joys that had been shattered by the coming of war. They never ceased in their efforts to cheer the men or to make each day at sea a little easier to live through, but the future and its secrets were always there, just at the back of the mind.

Rolling and yawing, the *Dorchester* beat her slow way north-eastward, unmindful of the comfort of her precious cargo. The cutters watched their brood with endless devotion and the ship's bells beat out their muffled count.

Somewhere up ahead, well north of the great circle route, in the impatient wilderness of the ocean, destiny was altering the *Dorchester's* course to a rendezvous with history.

II

~~~~~~~~~GEORGE LANSING FOX

~~~~~~~~~~~ The deep Pennsylvania valley stretched between the hills for miles. In winter it was like the crack of a crevasse through which the wind howled.

The Altoona railway shops—the largest in the world, the natives boasted—sprawled along the bottom of the valley. All day and all night the trains huffed and puffed over the maze of tracks. The air was always tainted with cinders. There was a compounded noise of hammers and shouting voices, of brakes and the slow chunk of starting freight trains.

Rows of drab houses perched all the way up and down the surrounding hills like drifts of dried leaves. The smoke made them all look alike in the end, one colorless color.

George Fox had time to ponder these things night and morning on his way to and from school. Life to him, even in his childhood, seemed a series of traps. There was first the big trap of the valley. To the north the Allegheny Mountains hemmed in the town; beyond the untidy rows of houses to the south, Luck Mountain rose up in the distance.

The secondary trap of the squeezed-in, smoky streets led to the ultimate trap of home. The house was an old two-family affair near the corner of Twelfth Street and Fourth Avenue, rising from the sidewalk ungraceful and boxlike. Two identical porches marred the front. Inside, a living room about ten feet square was the meeting ground of the family. Behind it lay the kitchen. From that point a curving flight of stairs in the wall led to the two bedrooms on the second floor and a further half-story attic. The front bedroom on the second floor was occupied by George's father and mother; his sister Gertrude had the back room. The four boys slept in the dormer-windowed attic.

The family lived at close quarters. When Mother was busy or at church, which was often, there was a loud clash of voices and personalities. But she had a passion for order and her children respected it. Their fighting stopped the moment they saw her dignified figure in the distance coming down the street. The fawn-colored voluminous dress reached her ankles, the black velvet bonnet topped her placid face and smooth, drawn-back hair.

Her Germanic placidity stood up under the most trying situations. *Stille,* she would say in a mild voice, or *Schnell,* but her will was a match for her placidity; it was hopeless to oppose her. She was like a general deploying her forces for a perpetual struggle with her husband. Such a little it took to arouse his Sicilian temper and the roughness of his voice. "You must not annoy Father," she would warn. "You know his leg hurts him."

The children could sense trouble in the ungainly swing of their father's artificial leg when he came home at night from the switchyard, scowling and grunting his way through the living room, clattering his dinner pail on the edge of the sink. The children had learned from experience that their father's hand was quick and heavy. Vaguely they understood that he often suffered, and his quick temper was largely the result of pain. It was his idea of discipline they couldn't grasp. It stemmed from old-country ways that believed children should be instantly obedient.

In his visits to other families George could contrast the casual character of American manners with the discipline expected of him in his own home. American ways seemed extremely desirable to George. It must be wonderful to be free, to think of nothing beyond finding amusement and pleasure. The carefree attitude of his schoolmates was a reproach to his own narrow round of duties.

The garden behind the house on Fourth Avenue stretched from the end of the narrow porch to a stone wall with a whitewashed picket fence. The boys were responsible for this patch after school was out. They weeded and hoed in a perpetual struggle to tend the precise rows of onions, carrots, radishes, tomatoes, peppers, and leeks. The work had to stand the scrutiny of their father. In this field, at least, he was an expert. He had a green finger and a love of the soil that came out of his own childhood.

[21]

Mother was always telling them how important the garden was. "It saves a little money for us. And your father wants to find a farm. He will be happier there. The switchyard doesn't agree with him, you know that."

Their mother led the conversations at supper in the kitchen. She knew how to quell a raised voice with a glance, and she retailed the small news of the neighborhood in a way that even brought a faint smile to their father's face.

When supper was over, Gertrude cleared the table and, with her mother's help, washed the dishes in the big pan. The boys were already at their homework in the small living room: four dark heads bent over books and tablets. They could hear Father clumping about in his room upstairs, getting ready to go out. Shortly he would come through the sitting room in his best black suit, his square hat set squarely above an unsmiling face.

Every night he went down to the South Side of town for a visit with his closest friends in an atmosphere where a *paesano* was something, and a man's native dignity was acknowledged without a certificate of Anglo-Saxon parentage or *Mayflower* origins.

He would come home early, usually at nine-thirty. The intervening hours were a time of freedom. If Mother went to church in the evening, the boys would rush through their school tasks and hurry out of doors. Under the street lamp the neighborhood boys were playing run sheep run. There was time for a few quick games. The signal for dispersal was the first sight of their mother's straight figure. They dashed into the house and resumed their studies until presently their mother said, *"Bett,* now!" They obeyed instantly; Father would expect them to be in bed when he got home.

In winter the attic wasn't too bad—the room was cold and

they were soon asleep. But in summer it was torture. The low
window was wide open, but the air was stale and hot. The four
boys squirmed and tossed. The shouts of the children at play
drifted up to them like rumors of some happy country from
which they had been banished. Bert and Leo accepted the stern
regime—they had their mother's placidity—but George and his
oldest brother, John, were always in secret rebellion. Why
shouldn't they play like the other children? George reasoned.
What was the sense of tossing in the heat while the sky was
still full of light? Lying there on his bed, George liked to fancy
himself in a strange land where trees were green and the air
was crystal clear. Free time there was really free—he could go
where he liked when he liked. He could play baseball to his
heart's content or just dream away the hours.

George's imagination was well stocked with the materials from
which dreams are made. At Fourteenth Street and Third Avenue
there was a free children's library. It was an unusual venture
started by a childless couple, the Kruezpointers. They were Pennsylvania Dutch and loved children. Out of their love and modest
means they had assembled a library of children's books in their
living room. Mr. Kruezpointer had old-fashioned mutton-chop
whiskers. Mrs. Kruezpointer was plump and red-cheeked. Children found it easy to talk with her. They fingered the books in
the cases, discussed possible choices, and listened to her advice.

George loved to go to the Kruezpointer library. The boy had
been thoroughly amazed at his mother's reply when he first
broached the subject to her.

"The Kruezpointers are fine people. It is good for you to read.
It makes a man smart. In Germany all my family were great
readers." She sighed. "Now there is no time any more, but God
knows best! I'll speak to your father."

For once George's father didn't object; he, too, took pride in seeing his children get advantages he had never had in Sicily. If George could obey the family rules and fulfill his duties, there was no reason why he shouldn't read as much as he liked. The boy had fine qualities—that couldn't be denied. He was bright and quick. The very best reports of him came from his teachers. He was helpful in the garden and liked to run errands for his mother. The paper route he had taken was another instance of his thoughtfulness.

Parental approval of the Kruezpointer library opened up to George the first gateway out of his private trap. In the adventurous lives of *Tom Swift* and the *Rover Boys* he saw the full possibilities of a life that was exciting and free. The priggish goodness of the heroes seemed perfectly natural to him. It was a goodness that came from within them and was not imposed by a stiff discipline that squeezed the joy out of living. At night the walls of the narrow living room seemed to fall down before the power of the boy's awakened imagination.

"You are reading fast. No?" Mrs. Kruezpointer would say to George when he came through the side door of the library in the early evening. She advised him and mothered him. Often, too, she would give him a few molasses cookies or a handful of peppermints. These were occasions for George. New books under his arm, he walked along the street like a man inspired.

School, too, was a welcome relief. He did well in his studies, particularly in reading and arithmetic. In history the character of Lincoln interested the boy. He read everything he could find on the life of his hero. The kindliness of the man was attractive, and his simplicity was refreshing. There was discipline and repose in that tall, gaunt figure.

George learned the Gettysburg Address by heart. The simple

words of the speech summed up the sacrifice of soldiers in a way that made George's spine tingle. In speech class George was often called upon to recite the piece. He would get to his feet shyly and slowly. "Fourscore and seven years ago," he would begin softly, but the moment he heard his own echo, he lost all consciousness of himself and his voice rang out confidently.

School seemed easy to George after the many rules of home. His teachers were good-humored and quick to commend him, but among his classmates there seemed no one to whom he could give his complete confidence. He could hear the titters when he opened his lunch pail and they saw his Spartan slices of bread eked out with big Italian chestnuts. Sometimes they said to him, "Monkeys eat chestnuts too"; or they capered about like organ-grinders. George pretended not to see them, but he blushed. It was the same hot blush that came when he saw the boys laughing at his mother's country clothes.

His differences intensified his pride. Nearly always he was buried in a book at recreation time. George preferred his world of imaginary achievement to the hazards of boyish cruelty—the wounding word or the wisecrack that brought his disabilities into the open.

He would sometimes walk home with the two Lynam boys, who were in his grade, but he walked along mostly in silence and told little about himself. Let them guess what he was or desired to be. As long as they didn't know, he could possess his soul in peace.

His feeling for religion, too, was changing. From his earliest days his mother had prayed with him, and one of George's first memories was the daily walk along the dusty street to the church. His mother had held his hot hand in her cool fingers, and

George appreciated the quiet, and the dancing lights in the colored windows.

Those first memories and prayers had grown into a quiet thoughtfulness. He savored the clean upthrust of his own petitions toward a heavenly Father Who had something of the coolness and color of his first introduction to religion. Now, in his middle teens, George felt that the finger leading him along the street was the finger of God.

Soon the boy knew that he would not be able to put up with the situation at home very much longer. His father was centering all his thoughts on acquiring a farm. George saw at once what that move would mean to him. His present life was bearable; school was exciting and most of the day he was away from his father's iron-clad rule. Moving to a farm meant that his father would ride herd on him all day and the whole summer long. And the end of high school would be the end of his education. Until he married or settled down on his own he would be chained to the land of his father.

At seventeen, his brother John cut himself off from the family group and went away to live his own life. If John could do that, George thought, he could too. In any event, he was determined not to be a farmer. He wanted an education; he wanted a home and a family he could love, and a career that satisfied his own ambition. He was tired of going his father's way, and the first moment any possible line of retreat opened he meant to take instant advantage of it. He was every bit as good a man as his brother.

In the pages of *Current Events* he studied at school in 1915, George found new excitement. The wars of the past, except for his interest in Lincoln, had been to him little more than a series of dates and dry facts. Now he was living in the midst of a real war. It might affect him, might give him a chance to escape from the threat of the farm. He could hardly wait to see the newspapers every morning, and he followed the war maps with mounting tension.

President Wilson issued a series of sharp notes and denunciations of German inhumanity. To George it seemed obvious that the Germans were evil. He reacted violently to the letters in the paper in which Americans of German descent justified German methods and force.

At last war was declared. Young men from Altoona flocked into the services. George could hardly concentrate on the necessary tasks at home and school. To leave the trap of the discouraged valley and the trap of home, to see strange places in the United States and on another continent—France, Italy, Germany itself one day! The very names of strange places glittered like the ornaments on a Christmas tree. His imagination had invested them with a romance incapable of realization.

George longed to be in the middle of the struggle. But how could he manage it? He had just come into his seventeenth year. His body was hard from work in the garden. Staring at his face in the mirror each morning before starting to school, the boy realized that he looked older than his years. The rigid framework of home had given him a serious appearance that might enable him to pass for twenty. But there were necessary documents to be obtained. He would have to declare his actual age. Perhaps he could persuade his mother to give her consent; perhaps she would say nothing if he misrepresented his age. Once he was in the service it wasn't likely he would be sent home, if he could prove his value.

A day of full determination arrived at last. George turned his fears over and over in his mind while he walked backward and forward in front of the recruiting office. Tightening his nerves, he walked in. The sergeant took his name and date of birth.

"Eighteen ninety-nine?"

George fought to keep his face straight. His stocky build gave nothing away. He was sure of that.

"Where's your birth certificate?"

"I was born in Mifflin County. I didn't know I'd have to have my birth certificate."

"O.K.," the sergeant said at last. "You can send for the certificate. Meanwhile, I'll ship you on to Columbus Barracks. Your health good?"

"My health's perfect!" George said in a loud voice.

"O.K.! The doc will settle that question in Columbus. Be here tomorrow morning with the other volunteers. You'll go out together on the train. You can send for your birth certificate today. You should have it when you enter, and it may get to Columbus soon after you do."

That last evening at home George could barely control the sparkle in his eyes and the nerves in his hands. Records had been poorly kept in the state of Pennsylvania. In the mining districts, birth and death were casual affairs. The hurried visits of the busy doctors gave them little time for keeping exact records. George was convinced he could safely claim to be a year or two older than he was. It would be hard to trace his family from Lewistown to Altoona, and if the Army authorities were curious beyond that, he felt sure his father would be far too angry to write an answer.

George looked around the house that night with hostile eyes. It would be his last look and he might never see it again. He didn't care. His limited wisdom told him that the cow left the calf when it was grown enough. Ties of family were ties of chance. You inherited them and had to make the best of what you got. But you didn't have to like them, once you could think for yourself. He felt mature, capable of looking after himself.

He wouldn't be lonesome for anything. That wasn't entirely true either. He knew he would miss the tranquil face of his mother and her confidence in God. She loved her children deeply. Of that George was sure. Her love had been constant in service and prayer. That would be his creed: to copy his mother in both virtues. He would become a living monument to her training.

In the morning George left the house as usual, his small stock of toilet articles hidden away in various pockets. Those and the clothes he wore on his back were all he took away with him from home. He walked into Altoona and met the motley group of young men at the recruiting station. They received their armbands, and marched to the railway station.

The train pulled out of the yards and climbed toward the famous Horseshoe Curve. There was an empty feeling in the pit of George's stomach. What lay before him? Would he be sent back to the valley? Could he get into the Army with the age set down on his birth certificate? His father would be furious with him. To come home again was unthinkable. As the trees and hills flashed by the window, George's determination grew. Now that he had cut the last ties that bound him to a life he no longer wanted, he must outface all the hazards before him.

George's worry about his birth certificate grew with the miles. At stations where the train stopped, more and more volunteers came aboard. Their obvious uneasiness revived George's confidence and, smiling, he made himself at home with them. Red Cross girls came through the train at every station; George gulped the hot coffee and swallowed the greasy doughnuts.

In Columbus Barracks the new life annulled the old. There was little doubt in George's mind that he would pass the physical examination. Yet when he stood stripped in the long line leading to the doctor who was going to examine him he felt his heart pounding. The man in line before him was either of Polish or German descent. His muscular development told of days in the coal fields and he was obviously proud of himself.

"You're pretty skinny," he said to George.

"I guess so."

"Maybe you won't make it."

"Maybe not."

"And look how hard your heart is beating. Must be something wrong with it." The big fellow gave a crooked grin. "See! My heart is quiet." He took George's hand and held it to his own chest. George could hardly feel the pulse beat.

"See, I told you." The man shook his tow-colored head. "There must be something wrong with you."

George could feel the sweat pouring out all over his body. He saw himself rejected, returning to Altoona. He saw himself wilted, trapped in the blaze of his father's anger.

Then the doctor started to examine the man before George, testing the young giant's reflexes, then with his stethoscope going over the well-muscled chest.

"Jump up and down."

"Sorry, son," the doctor said at last. "You won't fight in this war. There's something wrong with your heart."

George watched the boy turn away; his sagging shoulders gave some clue to his dejection.

Now it was his turn. He prayed: "Don't let me fail, God! Don't let me fail."

George's examination was brief. "You're in perfect health, son," the doctor said. "And there's not a scar on you anywhere. I hope you stay that way."

The sergeant who completed George's papers was brusque. "We have everything but your birth certificate. That may come along in a day or two from Lewistown. I'll stretch a point, kid. Sometimes these things are slow. Your father's name ain't here. You have a father, haven't you?"

George flushed a deep red. "Yes!"

"O.K! O.K! Keep your hair on. Get going and pick up your clothes!"

George was elated with his new outfit. Most of the olive-drab clothes were made for men of medium height and weight. It was in the outsizes that men suffered the worst fits. George at least looked like a neat orphan. Over and over he rolled the puttees about his legs until he could do the job with his eyes closed.

In a sense he felt grateful for all the disciplines of his life in Altoona. Other boys in his group found the new life galling. They were exhausted after route marches, and lonely for the comforts of home, but to George it was child's play to swing along the dusty road in column. His mind was free to make excursions into the imaginary future, his eyes were free to observe the delicate green on the trees and the blossoming fruit orchards bent over the edge of the roads.

In the evenings, when he was not on K.P. duty, there was a special joy in being free. Often George took out his khaki-covered New Testament and read the story of the life of Jesus. It called to his heart in a way no other story had ever done.

George's sergeant told him he was probably destined for the Ambulance Corps. "You seem a bit young for the infantry."

George squirmed. His birth certificate had not arrived, but he maintained that he had given his correct age. He realized that the sergeant suspected he was not telling the truth.

"I'd like the Ambulance Corps," George said. "I've always wanted to learn to drive."

"Maybe you won't at first, but there'll be plenty to do once we get to France. Anyway, in the Corps you won't get any cooties and maybe you can fix me up with one of them good-looking Red Cross girls someday."

George blushed. To him the Ambulance Corps was a kind of holy thing. He would be giving men in pain and anguish the cup of cold water Christ commanded, and he would be binding up wounds, not making them.

Soon he was sent to Camp Newton D. Baker. Texas itself was a revelation. The wide prairies and the devouring sky dwarfed anything George had ever seen. Though it was only the last week in May, the weather was already hot. In Texas, route marches were really something. The sweat rolled down into your shoes and made marching painful. The slightest wrinkle in a sock felt like a mountain of misery. Yet George was happy as he had seldom been before. The sergeant's prophecy had been correct. He was in Ambulance Company #1, Second Sanitary Train, doing what he wanted to do. He was learning to drive, and already he could change a tire in jig time.

There was a lot to learn. The men practiced first aid on one another incessantly and discussed treatment for shock, gas, and the care of shrapnel wounds with all the seriousness of a group of doctors at a medical convention.

The field maneuvers were harder. Under the fierce Texas sun they established emergency posts and first-aid dressing stations, maneuvers that called for precise teamwork. The canvas marquee was first set up. Instruments and bandages were unpacked.

Every man had his job, and each job had to be executed on the double. Sweat ran into George's eyes; his back ached and his feet hurt; but he forgot himself and kept his eye on the ball every minute.

While crawling along swiftly over the harsh ground in search of fake casualties, George often wondered how this work would seem under fire. Then death, his own death, would be the greatest hazard. He wasn't afraid. If God watched the fall of a sparrow from the roof top, He would not look unkindly upon men who were trying to do His work of consolation.

"You get thirty dollars a day once a month," the standing joke on payday had it. To George it seemed a large sum—he wasn't used to handling money of his own. But he appreciated its full value as few of his fellow soldiers did. He sent some money home to his mother and saved the rest for his own needs and the uncertain future. Occasionally, when the dark dropped down, he was lonesome for his mother and the family. He wondered if they missed him and spoke of him at the supper table. He could picture his mother in church, a rapt look on her face. She would be praying for him now with a special fervor.

In early November word got about among the men that they would soon be moving overseas. Unlike many other rumors, it proved to be true. That meant a dreary ride of five days to the embarcation center at Camp Merritt, New Jersey. George was happy in being able to see so much of the United States. Whenever the train stopped along the way the townspeople of even the smallest villages gathered to wave and cheer. Sandwiches, coffee, candy, and cigarettes were passed through the open windows. When there were long stops, the sergeants routed the men out of their lethargy and took them out for short marches or snappy routines of setting-up exercises.

George's three days at Camp Merritt were highlighted by a twelve-hour pass in New York. George gawked about the city. The tall buildings seemed even larger than he had imagined. Forty-second Street was jammed with servicemen, all hungry-faced for a taste of excitement.

The two remaining days were a nightmare of work: packing full marching kit, shining and cleaning rifles and equipment. The inspections were endless and the lines of men awaiting inoculation seemed interminable.

On the morning of December 3, reveille blew at four-thirty. The voices of the sergeants bellowed through the barracks. "Everyone out!" It was still dark, and the men hurried about their last tasks under the glare of naked lights. George gulped his steaming tin cup of coffee in silence. Altoona was never like this. His life was enlarging beyond anything he had ever dreamed possible.

George's quarters aboard the *Huron* were on C deck, not quite below the water line. He had never been on a big ship before and everything he saw about him seemed miraculous. But he didn't like the smell of the place—a compounded odor of bilge and too much living.

For the first day out George was hopelessly seasick. The *Huron* plunged in the choppy sea. Her pace was slow at first, but after meeting her escort and receiving sealed orders she took on speed and plowed through the black-green water. Her zigzag course exposed her to every mood of the winter sea.

By the second day George had found his sea legs. He recovered more through his will and fresh air than from the thousand-and-one remedies other men were trying in desperation. The ship became a veritable hospital. There were several cases of influenza and pneumonia aboard, and George volunteered to spend his time in helping with them. The holds stank with the smell of sick men. From time to time George managed to get up on deck for a breath of fresh air. That was the only real remedy to be found—gulping in sharp drafts while the sea spray slapped your face with stinging needles. All George's dreams of the ocean had been happy ones of blue water glorified with sun. Nothing had prepared him for this menacing waste, constantly in motion like the coils of a serpent.

Of all the men aboard he felt most inspired by the young Mennonites in the ambulance service. While others complained, they tried to be helpful. They made themselves useful everywhere. Their surety and tranquility seemed to stem from their consciousness that they were in the Lord's hands and not at the mercy of either the water or German U-boats.

Through the nightmare passage George noticed how the men on the *Huron* were all drawn together by their danger. Men normally sullen or self-assertive showed a kindness foreign to them on land. They trotted out worn jokes to encourage their shipmates during the daily lifeboat drills and they showed a sympathy with the sick which was sensitive to a degree. Their very gripes were an expression of their compassion. They damned Pershing and the A.E.F., Wilson and war—everything, in fact, but their fellow-sufferers.

Two of the men with pneumonia died in the course of the trip and were buried at sea. In the pale winter sunshine George went on deck with all the men who were well enough to watch the funeral. The flag-covered dead, draped in their weighted canvas shrouds, seemed more like sticks of cordwood than human beings. The chaplain looked pale and drawn while he squinted at his small black book.

"I am the resurrection and the life." The wind carried his words into the sea-worn distance.

At Brest, George staggered down the gangway of the *Huron*. The rhythm of the ship was still in his legs. The firm land under his feet seemed to roll and sway.

In a driving rain the weary men marched to the base camp, a sea of mud and discontent. The hospitals overflowed with influenza cases. It was something new in the way of diseases and the doctors worked to exhaustion trying to fight it. The suddenness of its course was discouraging. One minute a man seemed in perfect health, the next day he was in a raging fever and spitting up blood before he died.

It seemed to George that he grew from boyhood to manhood overnight. He thanked God for his good health. Every hour of the day was a struggle for someone else; he had little time to investigate the romantic possibilities his new life promised when he had entered the recruiting office in Altoona.

War killed men and twisted them, tore them away from home where circumstances had protected them and buttressed their weaknesses. It was a dirty business too—a life of mud and crudeness. Yet George thought he could see its necessity. If evil were to be allowed to dominate the world, then the lives of every single human being would be stretched out into a misery the soldier endured for only a short period of time.

The training in Texas now seemed child's play compared with the intensive work expected of the ambulance train in France. Pershing and the A.E.F. would probably move forward in the spring. The Kaiser's offensive would be met by the raw masses of American troops on the east front of Paris. Duty in the hospital, endless field problems, nights in the open. The cold of France was far different from his home mountains, George discovered. It was wet and seemed to penetrate into his very bones. Blankets and pup tents seemed no insulation against it. On many nights George turned and tossed on the hard ground. He remembered his bed in the attic at home as a thing of luxury.

Letters from home told him that the family had moved from Fourth Street to Juniata Gap. His father had been able to get the farm he had coveted for many years. George wondered if that would improve his father's temper. It would be hard for the boys at home, he felt certain of that. Whatever happened, whether he lived or died, he was determined not to return to the atmosphere he disliked. If he could make his own way at eighteen among groups of hard-boiled soldiers, there couldn't be much doubt that he'd be able to support himself in peacetime in a world that had forgotten the strain of war.

In April the Second Sanitary Train moved up to the eastern front in slow stages. The brief sight of Paris was exciting. The candles on the chestnut trees were pink and white and the sparkle of the April light brought out the beauty of streets and parks. Compared with Paris, American cities looked dingy and poverty-stricken. The streets were thronged with the soldiers of all nations, and the sidewalk cafés and amusement places were crowded with well-dressed women.

In early April Hindenburg had rolled his Hun legions down to the Marne. Once again the line had held. American troops and supplies were arriving in quantity. Soon there would be a turning back of the gray horde that threatened them all. Paris in the spring of 1918 was a city of hope.

It seemed a far cry from Paris when the Ambulance Train reached the front lines at Vetri La France. Wounded men were brought in at all hours from raids. George was horrified and sickened at the first sight of these victims of mass slaughter.

Men with torn faces, wounds that seemed to promise no possible hope of survival. Blood, pus, gangrene—the stench of the living and the dead. The men who came down from the lines seemed greater casualties than the wounded. Under the black of beards an inhuman grayness showed. Eyes were dazed and dead-looking. They slumped along the roads in ragged columns like refugees from hell. Vetri was not far from American General Headquarters at Chaumont, and, like all the neighboring towns, it was a mess. Dispatch riders rushed up on exploding motorcycles. The streets were jammed with cars and horse-drawn vehicles.

George had his first taste of bombing at the new camp. Dusk was falling as he walked slowly toward the improvised mess hall. A horse van was drawn up near the mess and men were unloading crates of canned goods. George's mind was fixed on food and his eyes were focused on the bright shaft of light from the cookhouse door. The open space was peppered with figures moving up for the evening meal. Suddenly the sky overhead throbbed with explosive noise. In the gray light three Fokkers swept low enough to show their iron crosses. A zigzag of machine-gun fire swept the moving men. Explosion after explosion rocked the area. The air was filled with a rain of flying earth and splinters. The two horses screamed with a terrifying, almost human cry.

The whole scene lasted only a few moments. George had fallen on his face with the others. There was a taste of mud and fear in his mouth. His spine vibrated. Then, in the ominous silence, he was on his feet running toward the wounded men.

His first experience of raiding planes made George fear them more than any other arm of destruction he encountered. You could hear the whistle of the shells and the crump of mortars.

These sounds gave you at least the illusion of a chance, and you had ample warning in raids and advances of all kinds. But in air warfare there was no warning at all. One moment you were wrapped in the illusion of safety, in the next the sky rained down death. It made him feel that there was no help in the earth or heaven.

George didn't have many free moments to think about new dangers. The Germans had completed their spring drive, and the Second Ambulance Train was constantly on the move. From Vetri La France they hurried on to St. Nicholas, Bois L'Evêque, and from bloody Liverdun Woods to Bois De Jure in early September.

All they had experienced, George felt sure, was a faint taste of the horror to come. At Bois de Jure it was whispered around that the American Army as a group was on the point of going into their first massive action. Roads were lined with camouflaged trucks and supplies of all kinds. Guns had the right of way and they went in a mountainous procession toward the Saint-Mihiel salient.

On September 11 the sky was shaken with the thunder of three thousand big guns. Under cover of this rolling barrage American soldiers leaped out of their trenches into a no-man's land of thick barbed wire and deep shell craters. The advance was steady and George and his associates sweated all day long in an atmosphere that was saturated with blood. There was no time for sympathy, no time to let the heart speak; only an endless procession of wounds that had to be stopped somehow.

Removing the wounded under fire was quite unlike anything George had prepared himself for. He found, to his dismay, that he had to concentrate his entire energies on holding the stretchers level. There wasn't a moment's time to think of danger. Men went down at your very side but you had to struggle on, you had to forget that you might be hit. There just wasn't time to heed the warnings, there just wasn't time.

By nightfall the four-year-old pocket had been pinched off. The Americans were jubilant. Such was the force of the American advance that the Germans were unable to make a strategic withdrawal. Thirteen thousand Germans had been captured, and a huge quantity of guns and supplies. The Americans had at last proved their mettle.

There was little opportunity for George to share in the victory. Victories meant casualties. His mind was depressed with the bloody scenes he had watched in the dressing stations.

The boy turned for comfort to his soiled copy of the New Testament. All his prayers were for peace, rather than petitions for his own protection. One thing he saw clearly: he didn't want his life to settle down into mere physical struggle and physical things. He was determined to spiritualize his existence, and he hoped with all the force of his young heart that he would be able to make his days count in the scales of love in which God weighed the world and the men in it.

A fresh offensive was under way all along the line from Belgium to the border of Switzerland. In the new plan of battle the American forces were not going to be able to repeat the first overwhelming success of Saint Mihiel. The terrain over which the Americans advanced reminded George of the hill country near Altoona. The Germans disputed every inch of the difficult way. The mounting casualties were proof that they knew exactly what they were doing.

Yet there was talk of peace in the air. One last big push might decide the war.

On November 10th George was helping to set up an advanced

dressing station at Giraucourt. A brick factory building had been cleared of refuse. It seemed to be an admirable dressing station out of the range of the big guns, which had been drawn back in the last eight days' fighting.

One minute George was rushing about in silence, intent on his work; the next moment he screamed without knowing it. A soldier shouted from the wide door, *"German planes!"* Everybody inside the building tried to run for the open. Those who couldn't make it huddled against the brick wall, George among them. The explosions came nearer and nearer. Suddenly a flash of lightning split the roof. George never heard the explosion.

There was a whiteness everywhere around him when he woke. He was clean; he was in a bed with sheets—real sheets. He tried to move. His back was a mass of fiery pain.

A cup of water was pressed to his lips. It was good. So cold.

"Try not to move!" It was a woman's voice. "You're going to be all right."

George tried to focus his eyes on the dim face.

"And the war's over, soldier. The Germans signed the armistice today. Everyone's celebrating."

The month in the hospital was the only celebration George wanted. It was wonderful to watch the autumn sun climbing up the wall, to have nothing to do but eat and sleep. And no more war.

The doctors and nurses told George they were surprised at his rapid recovery.

"You nearly broke your back, but you're really on the mend. Your spine is healing nicely. First thing you know you'll be back with your unit. We thought at first you were headed for home."

"Where am I?"

The chief doctor laughed. His mustache danced on his face.

"That's what we'd like to know. This is an evacuation hospital but we're on the move. You're at La Havre now. But not for long."

In a month's time George moved with the hospital train from La Havre to Le Mans. They finally settled in at Mesves in the south of France. The war-ravaged valleys of northern France seemed farther away than the valleys of the moon. George was anxious to get well as fast as possible. From the looks of the papers he read and the news he heard, the American Army wouldn't stay long on occupation duty in the towns along the Rhine. In what time remained of his foreign service George wanted to see a little of the country before he was sent home.

His insistence on daily walks and exercise, and his love of the outdoors restored him to his unit for light duty. The Second Ambulance Train moved up and down the Rhine from Nieder-bieber to Gross, stopping in the small towns en route. George observed that his mother's people seemed mild enough in their own country. They appeared soft-spoken and honest, and they made little gestures of amity toward the American soldiers bil-leted in their towns and homes. It was impossible not to like them, though George felt a threat in their very docility. It was at once their greatest virtue as a people and their greatest vice. They could be led anywhere. There was something sheeplike in the perpetual *"Ja, Ja!"*

Like all his fellows in the Army, George was anxious to get back to the United States. It would be good to hear again the old nasal twang in shops and trains instead of searching in his phrase book for slow conversation that made people smile.

He was feeling seedy again. His back pained him, and the doctor sent him for a week's rest to the base hospital during the last week of June in 1919. The doctors went over him with a fine-tooth comb.

"You're getting on fine," they said. "Of course you may have a little trouble with your back from time to time. But if you take it easy at first you should be as good as new in a few months."

George thought he detected a slight shift of emphasis. Officers, up to that point, had talked about the rewards of heroism as if they promised positive things. Now that George was really wounded and the war was over, he was strictly ex-hero. The emphasis fell largely upon his self-reliance.

He smiled wryly. This was at least realism. A man had to depend on himself. His consciousness of having done his duty was the only genuine reward he could expect. George thought back over the tough days of the last half year. The citation for his Silver Star said: "For gallantry in action against the enemy in the Champagne Sector." What dull words they were for the experiences he and his fellow soldiers had lived through.

Now he had a Purple Heart and the French *fourragère* and a far more glowing testimonial in the unit citation that he carried in his small box of papers. He read it over again from time to time:

"The 2nd American Division showed proof of the most admirable qualities of endurance and indomitable will to conquer during the course of the attack on July 18, 1918, southwest of Soissons. By their splendid efforts they surmounted many difficulties and, in the face of the enemy's deadly fire, performed the duties entrusted to them, thus contributing greatly to the success of the day."

"These units took a glorious part in the operations carried out by the 4th French Army in Champagne in October, 1918.

By their courage and endurance under fire at the attack of October 3d on Blanc Mont and the Medeah Farm, they took a large part in the advance of the infantry up to the outskirts of St. Etienne-à-Arnes. Thanks to the valuable assistance thus rendered to the infantry operations, the enemy was driven from the banks of the Suippe and from the Massif de Notre-Dame-des-Champs."

Already, George could see, he was history with those who lived on or were buried under the rows of crosses in a foreign land. Medals were not a dime a dozen, as some cynics implied. To the soldier they were small acknowledgments of tremendous realities. His own heart and memories alone could explain the full meaning of the ones he had earned. But his eyes were fixed on his future. The war had taught him the importance of peace; it had also given him some inkling of the tasks before him.

Return to Altoona did not suit his taste or his ambition. He wanted to serve people. In his heart there was no desire to bury his life on his father's farm under his father's discipline. He was determined to turn his religious life to some practical end, but for that he would need education which didn't seem easy to achieve from his present point of vantage. But Lincoln hadn't found it impossible; he had read and studied and had achieved the goals he had set for himself. George was determined to follow that pattern. He would work in the day and go to school at night. God would show him where he was needed, and in what way he could make his life count.

George went through the routine of separation from the Army in a sober mood. He wasn't going home, and he would require every penny of his savings and the bonuses the United States Government and the states were paying their discharged men.

He would need new clothes; he would have to support himself among strangers.

The verdict of the doctors in summing up his physical condition both amused and exasperated him.

"You're in pretty good shape," they said. "But your wound will kick up for a while. The Veterans' Bureau will see to any hospitalization you may need. And we'll certify 10 per cent disability. You'll get a pension for that, of course."

"A pension? How much?"

"Eight dollars a month."

"Eight dollars a day once a month," he said to himself. He couldn't call it magnificent, but it was sure—and it might pay for his night-school courses.

Getting a job proved easier than George had expected. He was neat and presentable in his new gray suit and hat. His Army papers and citations were so good that they forced employers to sit up and take notice.

His job with the Guarantee Trust Company gave him a fair chance to use his talent for figures. Every week his pay envelope held $25. It wasn't a fortune, but along with his pension and his savings the way was open for the realization of his ambition.

He had left high school near the end of his third year. There was still a full year of studies to be completed. The required nights seemed endless until he had mastered geometry and completed his courses in history and English. For recreation he went to the Y.M.C.A. His war experiences had given him a confidence in the good-natured advice of the secretaries he had met, and he still found them amiable and helpful.

George believed he had a call to preach. He felt an impelling desire to do so. Only in this way, he was convinced, would he be able to make his war experiences count in the cause of peace.

The faces of dying men haunted his dreams. They were like the voice of his own conscience urging him to do everything possible to make a better world.

It was clear to him that men were wrong-headed or evil because they hadn't fully accepted Christ and His plan for the world. If he, George Fox, could make men accept Christ without reservation, and could make men see the wisdom and peace in Christ's plan for the world, then George Fox would be playing the active part God had designed.

The quiet pattern of his days was made radiant with reflex light cast from his imaginary future. For the life he intended to live a wide education would be absolutely necessary. To preach without wisdom was to leave all the labor to God.

Through careful saving and by taking full advantage of his spare time, George was ready to continue his schooling in 1923.

After careful thought, he decided that Moody Institute in Chicago would be a good starting point. His friends at the Y.M.C.A. had agreed with him. At Moody he would be thrown in with a group of ardent evangelists. His own enthusiasm and love of the Gospel would be blown to full flame.

The Institute more than lived up to the promise. George studied the Bible, and learned to quote from it with fire and precision. In group discussions he found he could more than hold his own with the best of the students.

One student above all others stood out in all George's classes —a tall, dark girl whose verve and sparkling conversation completely captivated George. Others in his class had spirit; she had fire. Others spoke well; her preaching was electric and beautiful.

George was shy. Isadora Hurlbut seemed at first a star far beyond any orbit in which he could hope to shine. She was from

Hyde Park, Vermont, and her people were well-to-do farmers. Gradually he got to know her at classes, and he treasured the memories of those frequent meetings. One thing was clear to his heart—he was in love with her. But could he hope to be able to measure up to her talent and ideals?

For months he agonized over the question while their friendship deepened. Classes and meetings paled before the strength of his dream. Would she marry him? How wonderful it would be to have a wife who was herself a forceful evangelist! Then he could look toward a career of service which would widen out in ever-greater circles.

At last George plucked up courage to ask the question.

They drove down to Winona Lake in Indiana for the wedding. The radiant face of his bride at their wedding presaged the dawn of a new day for George; it was the pledge of a bright future.

In the autumn of 1935 George and his wife went to Vermont to begin their work together. During their courtship Isadora had tried to imbue George with some of the love she had for the state where she had been born. She had hundreds of stories illustrating the kindness of the Vermont people, their integrity, and simplicity.

Seeing Vermont for the first time with his own eyes, George found it the epitome of the childish dream he had dreamed long ago in the smoke and dust of Altoona: green hills, pure skies and quiet streams, forthright people.

Settling in at West Berkshire was the prelude to the evangelistic work. George had been appointed circuit rider between West Berkshire, Franklin, and East Franklin. His territory was right up against the Canadian border; a rough isosceles triangle with Lake Carmi in the center. West Berkshire was itself one

[47]

of the ports of entry from Canada. Life there was quiet, but interesting and varied.

George found in Charles C. Chayer, the district superintendent of the Saint Johnsbury district of the Vermont Conference of the Methodist Church, an evangelist of top stature. The "work of the Lord" was to Reverend Chayer not a mere phrase of lip service. The work of the Lord was the salvation of men; success showed itself in their lives and the strength with which they hated evil.

George plunged into the work of the ministry with fervor. Sometimes it seemed that he was forever on the road, consoling the sick, praying with the dying, visiting his people. In late spring and summer the work of preaching and friendly visits was a delight, but when the endless snows came and there was just barely one track on the road, it required fortitude and stamina to shuttle between the little meeting houses of his circuit. The wind bit into his face; the churches were often cold and draughty. Yet in winter most of his people especially needed the help of religion. They were walled in on themselves in an icy stillness. George's smile and his enthusiastic love of God brought a ray of the extraordinary into lives that had narrowed down to their own fields and small home concerns.

The work was brimming with consolations, however. After the coldest journey filled with the winter discomfort, there would be the smiling Sunday faces of people hungry for the word of God. They sang the hymns with genuine enthusiasm and a complete lack of the formality advised by the *Discipline* of the church. George let the spirit of the melodies—"Sweet Hour of Prayer", "Rock of Ages"—carry him away, and he was glad of the good voice the Lord had given him.

The lessons from the Old and the New Testament were a

table of wisdom. Then, when the last hymn was sung and the benediction had been said, it was pleasant to chat with the neighborly people; to discuss crops and village concerns; to lay plans for the further meetings and the extension of the Lord's work.

As a simple itinerant preacher George knew he was on trial before the Church. If he justified his call in the purity of his life and the worth of his service, he could look forward to the office of deacon or elder. It was gratifying to see with his own eyes the report in the *Minutes* of the annual conference of the Methodist Church, held at Enosburg Falls in the last week of April, 1927. District Superintendent Chayer had singled out George and five other circuit riders for special commendation in a witty phrase, "a three-point circuit rider." Chayer continued: "What circuit riders of any day surpass them in devotion?"

If this district superintendent, and the Church, found his work of value, George was happy about it, but less than satisfied with himself. The ministry was a high calling. If he meant to succeed in it, as he wanted to, he would require a wider education. All through his second year at West Berkshire, George laid plans for his future.

The demands on the Vermont educational fund were heavy. Congregations in the area were not large, and the educational offering, made once a year on "Children's Day," was not sufficient for the constant strain upon it. But the Church was resourceful. What George could not hope to obtain in the field he had chosen to work might be found elsewhere. Both he and Isadora had powerful friends in Chicago.

In 1929, after two years of successful circuit riding, George left the Vermont Conference and went back to Illinois. A student pastorate at Downs, Illinois, was made available to him. With this as a financial backlog George entered Illinois Wesleyan at Bloomington, Illinois, for the completion of his college studies. It meant rising while the morning stars were still bright in the sky, it meant hard work until late in the night, and the Sunday responsibilities of a parish, but George shouldered his tasks with a smile.

Looking back on his lonely vigils in France, he remembered how he had feared the difficulties of life. Now God had smoothed them away; He had opened a path before George's feet. His marks in his classes were excellent, and though he enjoyed the freedom of the Middle West, he still looked forward to the day when he would return to Vermont. In his reading he was always running across traces of the New England he loved; they made him nostalgic for the country he had known.

The bachelor of arts degree at Illinois Wesleyan was one step upward in his education. It gave him a knowledge of worldly wisdom, the classics, history, and an insight into men. But best of all it opened the way for him to go on to the Boston University School of Theology. In that pentecostal atmosphere he would be able to enlarge his study of the Scriptures, and lift his secular learning to a plane which would transmute its labored wisdom into intuitions of the spirit.

The Church was quick to aid his other-worldly ambition. Again a student pastorate at Rye, New Hampshire, provided the funds for living. Rye was beautiful in summer. The long beaches were bright with playing children who reminded George of his own son, Wyatt Ray. In winter, with a norther blowing, the town was gray and tired-looking, but his work for the church slacked off in those months of cold and snow. On winter days at home he had more time for studies, and hours for meditation in sight of the sea, itself a figure of eternity.

In 1932 George received a practical and spiritual measure of his success. The annual conference was at Waterbury, Vermont. The spring flowers still lingered in the forests and along the edges of well-cut lawns. George was presented to the Church Assembly for the usual interrogation that went with the office of deacon.

The Sunday solemnity of the occasion lingered in George's mind with echoes from the Collect: "Almighty God, who by Thy divine providence has appointed divers Orders of Ministers in Thy Church, and didst inspire Thy Apostles to choose in the Order of Deacons Thy first martyr, Saint Stephen, with others: mercifully behold these Thy servants, now called to the like Office and Administration; so replenish them with the truth of Thy doctrine, and adorn them with innocency of life, that both by word and good example they may faithfully serve Thee in this Office to the glory of Thy name, and the edification of Thy Church, through the merits of our Saviour Jesus Christ, who liveth and reigneth with Thee and the Holy Spirit, now and forever. *Amen.*"

The vibrant voice of Bishop Anderson was asking George the first question: "Do you trust that you are inwardly moved by the Holy Spirit to take upon you the office of the Ministry in the church of Christ, to serve God for the promoting of his glory and the edifying of his people?"

"I trust so. . . ."

The bishop's hands were on George's bent head, at length, and the words flowed out above him, "Take thou authority to execute the office of Deacon in the Church of God; in the name of the Father and of the Son, and of the Holy Spirit. Amen."

The bishop held out the Bible. George put his hand on it and heard the solemn admonition: "Take thou authority to read the Holy Scriptures in the Church of God, and to preach the Word."

What had been achieved was massive encouragement to continue toward the office of elder. The end of the ministry was in sight. In 1934 the day came at last, bringing with it a fullness of heart and mind such as George had never envisaged in his happiest dreams.

His examinations were over at Boston University. He was ready to graduate with his class on June 11, the day after his ordination.

His ordination as elder took place in Barre, June 10, where the annual conference was in session. George drove far into the night in order to get back to Boston. Tomorrow he would be a full-fledged pastor of the church with the added authority of a bachelor of theology. His sudden eminence made George feel humble. What good was learning of the mind unless it was transfigured by the lessons of the Gospel? His work remained the same—to lift his people; to realize for them goals they could only dimly see; to re-direct their ambitions and lives in the spirit of love.

Driving down to Boston, after the ordination ceremony, George recalled, even more than the laying of the hands and the solemn charge of Bishop Burns, the words of the *Veni Creator,* which had been spoken as a dialogue by the bishop and the elders while he knelt before them:

> Come, Holy Ghost, our souls inspire,
> And lighten with celestial fire.
> Thou the anointing Spirit art,
> Who dost Thy sevenfold gifts impart.
> Thy blessed unction from above
> Is comfort, life, and fire of love.

[52]

Enable with perpetual light
The dullness of our blinded sight;
Anoint and cheer our soiléd face
With the abundance of Thy grace;
Keep far our foes, give peace at home;
Where Thou art Guide, no ill can come.

Teach us to know the Father, Son,
And Thee, of both, to be but ONE;
That through the ages all along
This may be our endless song:
Praise to Thy eternal merit,
Father, Son, and Holy Spirit.

George had already been appointed pastor of Waits River, a circuit in the heart of the maple-sugar country. The village was quiet and out of the beaten path. The clapboarded church, painted white, stood next to the post office. The frame parsonage was roomy and comfortable, with a pleasant living room looking out on the main road.

George threw himself into the circuit work. In a matter of days he was chatting with everyone in the village. The reticence of the natives found something appealing in the shy kindliness of the new pastor. He went about his business in an easy fashion. His circuit took in the meetinghouses at East Orange and West Topsham, and the minister was forever on the road. Slowly he broke the ice with a discussion of their own interests: the crops, the children, the prospect of good sugaring. But once he had established himself in their confidence George tried to make them conscious of the world of the spirit and their responsibilities in it. They all knew he was a man of learning, and they were grateful that his learning was not obtruded on them. In his sermons the new minister used graphic illustrations taken from country life, and he brought the Bible alive in simple stories that spoke the language of the heart.

In the summer Bible School George proved to be an interesting teacher. Classes in drawing and handiwork enlivened the sessions. The children found George quick and humorous; they appreciated him all the more, in that his humor was not of the joke-book type but flashed out of occasions like their own.

The two years spent in the Waits River circuit were a quiet introduction to George's next pastorate in Union Village. The brick church in Union Village was about a hundred years old, set back from the street in its own grounds. Seen from the road, it had both dignity and charm. The houses of the villagers straggled along on both sides of the road that ran through the narrow valley. It was an old and settled congregation, not given to much speech. Strangers settling in the town might consider the atmosphere chilly at first, but the moment sickness or sorrow touched them a real spirit of love flowered. Gifts of food and offers of financial help came pouring in, and differences of creed were never once thought to be impediments to giving.

George's survey of the boundaries of his big parish made him feel that it was a field ripe for harvest. Yet he saw at once that there was much work to be done. The people of the lonely parts of the district, like most dwellers in long-settled places, had let their church attendance become perfunctory and occasional. George was determined to make a valiant effort to alter that condition. After some labor he got permission to use the five schoolhouses in the district for a week at a time. He went to each in turn. A portable melodeon was in the back of his car. After the lamps were lit, the assembled congregation sang hymns until the rafters shook. George launched upon the sermon with an enthusiasm that was contagious; his prayers had

[54]

a fervent spirit that brought his hearers to confess their faults and seize salvation.

By the time he had completed the series of meetings the whole district was talking about religion, and, better still, the people were living with a renewed consciousness of God. Church attendance at Union Village and East Thetford jumped, study groups were started, the women were all busy with foreign mission work.

In the late summer the people flocked to the church hall for the big social of the year. It was called "Sugar on Snow." The church grounds were crowded with cars, the hall was bright with the summer silks, the children gorged themselves with the brittle sugar, cold as the crushed ice on which it had been ladled.

In the successful summer Bible School the young people struggled with Bible study, and they found amusement and relief from serious concerns in painted and burnt-wood mottoes and plaques made with their own hands.

George was content with the tranquil security of his home life. He had two children now, Wyatt and Mary Louise. His daughter had been born during the West Berkshire pastorate. Wyatt was brilliant in his schoolwork; his steady progress was a tribute to his father's amiable guidance. George was determined to lead his children and not demand their obedience. His own childhood had demonstrated the futility of obedience without love.

There were times when his old wound bothered the minister, but on such occasions Isadora was there to take his place on Sunday. George knew that many people preferred her sermons to his own, but he was pleased that it should be that way.

George's nearest neighbor was Mrs. E. O. Randall. The Randalls were comfortable farmers and had the kind of quiet cheerfulness George admired. He often dropped in at the Randall home for a brief visit. Sometimes in the evening Mrs. Randall would play the hymns he loved. George found in her Christianity a refreshment of his spirit.

He was sorry to leave Union Village, but his sorrow was tempered by the rich opportunities in the wider field to which he was called in Gilman, Vermont, a mill town on the Connecticut River. From the towering brick chimney of the mill the streets of the town fanned up over the hill in every direction. Most of the property, George found, was owned by the mill. He would have to live in a mill house, but the one he rented was a neat frame building freshly painted. It was commodious and pleasant, and only a short walk from his new church.

The church charmed George the first time he saw it. Behind the chancel the windows were of stained glass with a cross motif. On the sides of the room the small-paned windows of clear glass came almost to the floor and through them he could see the masses of mingled pine and birch trees in which the church stood. On sunny Sundays in winter when George looked out over the assembled heads of the congregation he was enchanted with the refraction of green light that seemed like perpetual summer. It was a Beulah-land atmosphere that evoked something special in the way of religious feeling. The grove was always filled with birds, even in winter. Their sharp calls sometimes rose above the tones of the organ.

The people of Gilman differed radically from all those George had met in his earlier pastorates. They were less silent, less reserved, more humorous. George made a practice of waving to the men on the street as he met them going to and from their work in the mill. The men seemed to like that. They appreciated his slow smile and his neighborly habit of stopping in the street for a moment's chat with them. In Gilman, too, George found that he could give some rein to his native sense of humor.

When the women of the church gave a tea confined to women only, George picketed it with a large sign which said, "Unfair to the Men of the Parish." The town appreciated the touch. They were used to seeing pickets and signs, and George's action showed that he was one with them.

The work of the church prospered in the societies; attendance at Sunday worship was good in both Gilman and East Concord. Those were healthy signs of progress, but George was determined to carry his belief out into the world his people lived in. He was convinced that religion failed unless it touched every aspect of life. A minister might fancy that things went well enough if he only felt the pulse of his people on Sunday morning, but he was merely fooling himself. Vital religious movements had always been strongly rooted in the lives and actions of men. The men of Gilman were the key to the problem. As long as they left religious concerns to their wives and children, religion would lack the vital strength that made it effective.

In pursuit of his goal George joined the Walter G. Moore Post of the American Legion. It was composed of men of all religions and all shades of opinion. In accepting the minister's application the men probably expected to be constrained by his presence at their meetings. Beer was sometimes served at Legion parties, and the men played endless games of cribbage. Any fancied feeling of constraint vanished at their first meeting with George. At once he made himself useful to them in countless quiet ways. If a legionnaire was sick, George called on him, not with formal phrases of religious consolation but in the hope of doing something immediately practical. Men who lived on weekly wages couldn't afford to be ill. George pulled wires and got them into the Veterans' Hospital; he high-pressured the Veterans' Bureau in Montpelier for pensions or increase of pensions if he was convinced they were warranted.

"Leave it to me, I'll take care of it," George promised.

His services to the men of the Post was of such high caliber that his name was soon brought to the attention of the Veterans' Department in Montpelier. The top officials and secretaries had seen him coming in and out on errands for the sick. His work was outstanding and it merited reward. George was surprised but not displeased when he was appointed State Chaplain of the Legion. For a time he was also State Historian.

His blue Legion uniform looked well on him. In convention parades he wore his medals. His fellow legionnaires in Gilman were proud to see their chaplain honored. He deserved it, they felt, not only for what he was to them but for his achievements in World War I. George joked with them about his experiences in France, but his very reluctance to give himself the status of hero was one more good mark in his favor among the men. Here was a man who understood them. George's stocky, erect figure was a welcome sight at any gathering. Whether the men were of his faith or not, every one among them relished his genuine interest in themselves and their problems. He had sympathy in abundance, but it was something more than sympathy. He ranged himself with them and identified himself with their struggles and ambitions.

George was dismayed at the beginning of the war in Europe. As he listened on the radio he couldn't doubt that America would be forced into the struggle. Most of the men at the Post all felt the same way. They argued loudly, but at heart they were all convinced that America couldn't sit out the war.

Often, in the evening, George went into the church to pray.

He knew what war meant—the scars of its meaning were on his body. But he was a man of peace and he tried to puzzle out God's purpose. Outside the thrushes were singing their evening song. Why couldn't men live at peace with one another? George asked himself. The evening quiet gave no answer. The colored motto above the arch of the chancel offered a possible clue. "Jesus the Light of the World," it read. That was it. Wars were the result of man's failure to accept that light. They preferred the darkness of evil and their own selfish roads to money and power.

At Post meetings George was often upset by a kind of new intemperateness among some of the men. The mill workers for the most part were with President Roosevelt, but the Commander of the Post was a rock-ribbed Republican and he and several of his close friends despised the President and all his works.

On one occasion when the Post Commander was talking with special bitterness against President Roosevelt, George found his temper rising. The moment the last word of the speech was finished he rose from his chair. The silence in the room was electric. Obviously the minister was going to say something important.

"Mr. Commander, this subject has gone beyond all bounds of patriotic tolerance. We're supposed to be a patriotic organization—a military organization. And whether we like Mr. Roosevelt or not, we ought to remember that the President is our Commander in Chief."

George spoke the words swiftly but without heat. He sat down amid an explosion of applause.

After Pearl Harbor George was torn between his duty and common sense. He had fought through one war. No one expected him to fight another. How hard he had worked for his education only he and his wife really knew. It wasn't sensible, considering that struggle, to think of risking his future in the chaplain service. Besides, he had been certified 29 per cent disabled in 1939, and his pension had been raised to conform with his new status.

The more George prayed and thought, the more he was convinced that his own heart would force him to enlist. The newscasts on the radio were lit with flashes of hope, but the casualty lists in the papers were long and disturbing. Every man would be needed. Men of God above all! His own first hand acquaintance with camp life and army ways could be of some use to his country and his church. It had been a hard road that led to his present standing in the Church. But in offering all that he was to God and his country, he wasn't giving one iota more than the young men who wagered their entire future in the struggle.

As a climax of all the doubts that beset him, he and his son Wyatt went the same day to enlist. Wyatt was taken into the United States Marine Corps.

In official eyes George was well prepared to overcome the handicap of his physical disability or what remained of it. His application was buttressed by letters from distinguished men. Arthur Wentworth Hewitt had long been his close friend, a man of might in the Methodist Church in Vermont. It made George's heart glow to read the summary of Hewitt's letter to the Methodist Commission on Chaplains: "He is genuine, sincere, and attractive. He is friendly and adaptable and is a pastor who has added to the church in four years 127 members in two country parishes."

Commander Casey of the Vermont Legion widened the picture in his recommendation: "During the service of World

War I he not only gained the tolerance of other faiths, but his service was also a credit to him."

Governor Willis' letter added a resounding period to the testimony: "He was especially successful in youth work." Few chaplains who applied to the Commission on Chaplains had George's exceptional recommendations, or his wide record of service.

Any doubt George had that he might be turned down by the doctors was resolved in his first physical examination at Fort Ethan Allen. Major Lewis did the probing, and his report to George was favorable: "You're in, Padre. I'm perfectly willing to certify you for any kind of service."

George was jubilant. How different it was from his experience in World War I. Then he had been a runaway boy who had quaked in terror while he waited in line before the examining doctor.

It pleased George to be assigned to the Chaplains' School at Harvard. The uniform felt good, and George found it a mind-widening and heart-lifting experience to meet men of diverse faiths intent upon the one end of serving God in helping their country. George went down to call on his many friends at Boston University; Vermont was near enough to visit, even on short leaves. Letters from Wyatt were encouraging. That took a great weight from George's mind. He wanted his son to be happy, and he realized that boot camp for the boy would be a hard grind.

George's first assignment to the 411th Coast Artillery Battalion at Camp Davis was in the nature of a disappointment, which he kept to himself. In the Coast Artillery he might sit out the war in comfort. Let the world think that if they wished to think it. The real war, George knew from experience, was against sin and evil. This was total war indeed, but the real front was in the hearts of men. They needed to be uplifted; they wanted guidance—man-to-man discussion of their problems, and active help in their weakness.

So successful was George in his new ministry that his transfer to Camp Taunton came as nothing of a surprise to him. He was going to see foreign service after all. That the station assigned should be Greenland made him chuckle a little to himself. His own hard life had mad him better prepared for that hitch than any of the other chaplains who were going with him. He was used to snow, and the quiet in which the language of the heart could make itself heard. Like his friend Alex Goode from the Harvard Chaplains' School, Clark Poling and Father Washington were city boys. The assignment would be difficult for them—his confreres all looked fit, they were full of ambitious plans, but the atmosphere of Greenland would be far harder for them to bear than it would be for him.

During his final leave George was oppressed by the irrevocable character of his parting visits. The dark pines and the wide white fields of Vermont seemed to salute him with a voiceless farewell. His life was repeating itself. In World War I he had entered service in May; he had entered this war in the same month. Now he was taking ship in winter again. What was in the unknown that yawned before him?

III

all ways thinking of melk out

~~~~~~~~~~ALEXANDER D. GOODE

wwwwwwwwwww The sun in the west hung like a red ball over Jersey. On the Brooklyn streets the light was still lively, and the voices of children shrilled on the pavements after a day at Coney Island . . . happy children . . . the red cheeks of the Irish . . . the tanned olive skins of the Italians, and the Jewish boys and girls. They carried damp bathing suits and sandy milk bottles in which they had brought sea water to wash their feet before the ride home on the subway.

In Myrtle Avenue the windows of one small house were already faint with light. Neighbors leaned over the fence talking to one another in undertones. The wailing of an infant could be heard—the voice of a newborn child.

Along the street came a hurrying figure, short, stocky, with a ruddy face full of kindness, a clipped mustache. There was intentness and concern in the face. The man bent over to un-latch the gate of the house where the lights glimmered. In that moment he was surrounded by a little crowd of women and men.

"She is all right? Yes?"

"Yes, fine—fine, everything went well. An easy delivery, they say. Thanks to God!"

"And the baby, Rabbi?"

"A fine, bouncing boy. Listen to that yelling. Good lungs, no?"

Easy laughter rippled across the lifted faces. One bearded man put out a thick finger and tapped the rabbi's chest. "A boy, eh? I'll bet that pleases you."

Rabbi Goode drew up his shoulders. Little creases of pride and merriment sprang into his placid face.

"Ja, a boy! It pleases me, all right. But what else did you expect?" He thumped his chest and shared in the laughter. "We are a family of first sons. Always it has been that way."

A small silence. Men and women in the group sorted out their own memories of sons and daughters—hopes, deaths, disappoint-ments, triumphs.

"We didn't know," one withered woman volunteered. "We seen you run to the station and Mr. Klein thought——"

"Mr. Klein thought! He shouldn't exert himself." There was renewed laughter. "Naturally, I wanted Papa to know I had a son. So I sent him a telegram to Kingston, North Carolina, and I asked him to come for the *briss*. He'll come all right, I'm sure."

"What name will you give him?" The man with the beard questioned.

"Alexander David. Just like Grandpa."

"Maybe he'll be a rabbi too."

"No, I think not," Rabbi Goode said with decision. "God knows. This is a great new country. He will build bridges maybe, or a skyscraper. I want him to do big things. We have many rabbis now."

They all nodded. He had made their own dreams vocal. Something of their hope and pride shone in the faces they turned toward the dignified, energetic figure hurrying into the house.

Up and down Myrtle Avenue there was a flurry of interest in the new child. Neighborhood women trotted in and out of the house, clucking in admiration at the infant. "Such a pretty baby . . . such lovely blue eyes and black hair he's got over his head already."

"And the grandpa's coming for the name day, just like the rabbi told us. Coming all the way from North Carolina too."

Inexpensive gifts multiplied on the hall table for eight days. In spite of their lack of monetary worth, they told the story of love and neighborly kindness which blossomed along Myrtle Avenue.

Early on the morning of the eighth day the ceremony was completed. Now the new child was a part of that age-old covenant which Abraham had made long ago with God.

The boy's father with misted eyes spoke his thanksgiving and joy:

"Blessed art Thou, O Lord our God, King of the universe, Who hast sanctified us with Thy commandments and enjoined upon us the circumcision. And the boy's name shall be Alexander David."

Dreams of past greatness and future promise. Like Alexander, the whole world was before this boy, and all the people hoped for him something of the courage and humility of Israel's ancient king and singer.

Their nervous joy lent a particular hilarity to the feast spread on the table in the living room. They toasted the child's future with little sips of heavy, fruity wine and recalled the glories of their own family history, lustered tales they had all heard over and over again. In the retelling they had acquired the patina of old bronze or the sheen of the hand-woven silk they long had kept in fragrant chests for grand occasions.

Then Myrtle Avenue flowed in upon the family to congratulate them. The neighbors, too, shared in the feast. Alex could truly say of the day that he was a son of Abraham and a man of the people.

The first memories of the boy were of simple things such as the yellow color of the kitchen floor on which he played and crept and where when the weather was fine he seemed to be swimming in a pool of sun.

He recalled, too, the loud tick of the clock and his insistence that his father hold him up to watch the slow-moving pendulum and the pattern of wheels and gears. The clock was like a live thing—counting, always counting, whirring and grinding the minutes away into shreds of the past.

Some things Alex didn't remember at all, but the family liked to recall them with a chuckle. On one occasion—Alex was about four years old at the time—he was playing in the yard. A sudden thunderstorm threatened. The colored maid who was helping about the house went to the front door and called to the little boy to come in. He didn't want to, but the maid insisted. Once inside, Alex's voice piped above the crackles of the thunder: "Some bad angel is crabbing at God. Maybe He wants to sit outside."

Alex was not long the sole focus of attention in the household. Soon his brother Joseph was born. Strangely enough, Alex felt no sense that his nose was out of joint. The baby face of Joseph fascinated him. "God had sent him a playmate," his father said, "but always Alex must remember he was the first born and the head of the family."

He did remember it; he recalled it with more maturity and force when Moses was born, and again when Agatha came to complete the family group.

Far more than the events and persons of his first years Alex remembered the whole atmosphere of his home. It was a magic island governed by peace and love. Voices were raised only in laughter. Always there was the revelation of the week-end Sabbath. First the nose received the good news. Mama Fay bustled about the kitchen. The odors of baking and cooking scented the whole house. Then the house would be thoroughly cleaned and the floors washed and polished.

Last of all her hands flew over the silver candlesticks until they glittered in the dying light. The table was laid with sweet-smelling linen, the candles were a little tower at one end of it, and the twin loaves of twisted *hallah* and the silver *Kiddush* cup, filled with wine, made a brave show.

Everything was ready at last. Wide-eyed the children watched the lighting of the candles. The flames flickered for a moment or two, then shot into twin spears of fire. The mother stood watching the glow. They knew she was praying. Her hands spread over the flames were for a moment blood roses with the reflection of divining light. Raising her hands before her face, Mama Fay prayed:

"Blessed art Thou, O Lord our God, King of the universe, Who has sanctified us by Thy commandments and commanded us to kindle the Sabbath lights." Almost in a whisper she added, "May our home be consecrated, O God, by Thy light."

Afterward the children would crowd in the window that looked out toward the gate. Would father never come? It was hard to wait for the feast. The moments seemed endless, the voice of the clock dragged.

They recognized that energetic walk. At last he was coming. They rushed to the door to meet him. His smile, tinged with solemnity fitting the day, was a blessing in itself. *"Shabbat Shalom,* Father! Good Sabbath!" they greeted him.

Now he was washing his hands—a long, deliberate minute. At last they gathered near the table to sing:

> Welcome, Sabbath Angels,
> Angels of peace.

They were all smiling while Papa recited the passage from Proverbs in praise of Mama Fay: "A woman of valor, who can find? for her price is far above rubies." Their childish lips silently followed the passage to the end.

The *Kiddush* cup in Papa's hands gave off sparklets of light from the candles while he asked the blessing. They tasted the wine briefly and savored the bread dipped in salt.

When their father had blessed them all in turn, the real feast began. It was always different and exciting. Sometimes they sang songs. Then they asked Papa questions. He answered them all, and he told them stories out of their past: of David and Saul, Solomon and Judith. Angels of the Lord walked in and out of the fascinating tales. The children were happy and excited at bedtime. Their dreams were colored with the exotic stories of the evening.

The Sabbath day itself was less exciting. Always Papa tried to carry on the mood of exaltation from the night before. But it was not a simple thing to keep small hands quiet, to still the squirming of small bodies. God had rested after six days of labor, but for children the hush and the quiet were sometimes not easy to bear with complete satisfaction.

They saw the Irish and the Italians batting out flies in the sandlots; they heard the high-pitched, joyous voices shouting to one another on the way to Coney or the movies.

Light, God, rest . . . in time they came to appreciate this wisdom.

Toward evening the four children scanned the sky for the first stars until at last they swam out of the pale dusk like silver fish. "The Sabbath is over! The Sabbath is over!" The family gathered again about the table, wishing each other a happy week. The lights of the house were turned on for the hard business of living until the next Sabbath.

The feast of the Sabbath and the High Holy Days threw a net of glamor over life and living, evoking the best in the family. Dedication, heroism, achievement! They were proud, too, that they were self-reliant and imaginative like all their forebears.

Sometimes self-reliance overstepped itself. One night Papa brought home a big bag of seeds. "This year I'm going to have a real garden," he exulted. Alex was fascinated. The family sat about the dining-room table. The packets went from hand to hand. Red cabbage for the borscht they all loved, succulent onions and radishes, asparagus and leeks. The garish packets promised delights which set the saliva flowing.

The next evening Rabbi Goode looked on the mantel where he thought he had laid the packets, then in the cupboard and the sideboard. "My seeds," he questioned at last. "Where are my seeds?"

Alex came running. He caught his father's hand. "Come with me, Papa. I'll show you." Out along the narrow walk they went to the edge of the shed at the back of the yard. There was a sign of freshly turned earth—a small hole.

"See, Papa," Alex said in triumph. "Your seeds are here. I planted them for you so you won't have to work so hard."

"I didn't know whether to scold him or praise him," Rabbi Goode confesses.

Another instance of self-reliance did not pass unblamed.

For a long time Mama Fay had promised the children a day at Coney. They all looked forward to it with ill-concealed impatience. The weather had been sweltering all week and the nights brought no relief from the heat. The children's questions multiplied like guinea pigs—"Mama, when will we go to Coney? Tomorrow?"

Tomorrow and tomorrow. Another brassy-skied day.

"Today you needn't ask me questions," Mama said at breakfast one morning. "We are *going* to Coney." They helped her pack the basket with the bathing suits and the lunch.

At last they rumbled across the island on the subway. Alex insisted on carrying the heavy basket. He was seven; he must help his mother.

The fresh sea air was heavenly; the music of the merry-go-rounds and the turning, gaudy wheel with its swinging seats, the barkers from the side shows—noises which could lift a child's heart.

It was a day Alex never forgot for many reasons. The breezy boardwalks. The cool sands and the rushing babble of the waves. The sting of salt in his eyes. He loved this world of tossing water. It was a new element, enchanting, teeming with light. It stirred him with a sense of destiny.

Mama denied them nothing. They waded in the water and rode the merry-go-round. She bought them frozen custard and took them to see the freaks and the snakes.

The smaller children were worn to a nubbin of complaint by five o'clock. "We must go home," Mama said. She glanced at the sky with apprehension. Out over the ocean tremendous thunderheads were gathering. Already people were moving away from the beach—a thick stream of tired humanity flowing toward the black cavern of the subway station. Mama was carrying the basket now.

It was not until the train moved out of the station that Mrs. Goode discovered Alex was missing. Where had she lost him? In the crowd at the station or in the press at the door of the train? He was able to take care of himself, she knew. He had his fare in his pocket, but she worried just the same. Children were never secure anywhere these days.

Safe at home with the smaller children, she worried even more. A tremendous storm broke. The water came down in a cloudburst, and the angry sky was torn apart with the chains of the forked lightning. Would Alex be out in the storm, she wondered.

When her husband came in shortly after six o'clock, she confided her worries to him. "I wouldn't worry, Mother," he reassured her. "Alex has grown up on these streets. He can take care of himself. He'll be home."

The rabbi's words were justified. Alex bounced into the house about seven o'clock. "Papa," he cried, "I lost Mama at the subway station. Then the rain came, but I didn't get wet. I sneaked into a nickelodeon and when the rain stopped I came home. All by myself!"

Later in the evening Rabbi Goode took Alex aside. "It is a good thing to be self-reliant, my son, but it is a bad thing to worry your mother. When you go to Coney with her again, or anywhere else, for that matter, you must see that you stay together." The expressive face of Alex showed a touching sorrow and repentance. "This time there *was* some excuse," his father added out of pity. "It was a new experience. The storm, too, was unexpected. But you and I are the older men of the family and we must look after Mama and Birdie."

"I'll try," Alex promised.

He did try, and he succeeded, because he saw all things with a sensitive heart. His reports from school were excellent, and when the Hanukkah candles made the house radiant, Alex was one of the first to complete his words in the game of Hebrew anagrams which the children loved to play at this season.

Alex helped his mother now each Sabbath, polishing the candles, cleaning and dusting the house, gathering sprigs of green for the table. . . .

One evening Rabbi Goode came home later than usual. His face was alight with smiles. "Good news! Good news!" he announced after they were all seated at the table. "We are going to move to Washington." He looked at the unbelieving faces. "You're surprised, eh? Well, so am I in a fashion," he added with humor. "I have accepted the invitation of the synagogue in Georgetown to be their rabbi. Now Alex can be a senator."

The change to Washington was significant to Alex, far more important than his imagination had pictured that night at the table. Though the city had its rundown and tough neighborhoods cheek by jowl with splendid government buildings, there was a sense of the country about it which had been lacking in Brooklyn. In little squares and great circles the woods and fields invaded the town with splashes of green. Graceful old elms drooped long sprays along the parkways; sycamores, tulip and magnolia trees. Riders flashed along the bridle paths of Rock Creek Park, and out Cabin John way the waters of the Cumberland Barge Canal mirrored the honeysuckle-covered banks.

The contradictions of the city interested Alex as he came to know them at firsthand. The house on Tenth Street was in a neighborhood which had not yet learned co-operation and tolerance. In his first year at school Alex literally had to fight for his education. Among other risks, there was a vendetta between the colored boys of the neighborhood and the white boys. Perhaps it sprang less from lack of tolerance than from the thirst for raw excitement and the gang spirit active in most boys on the edge of their teens. With his brother Joe, Alex endured the varying fortunes of a war not of their making. Leaving the sanctuary of home, the two boys—hair slicked and faces shining—would enter the hazard of the street. They were much alike in many ways. Both had thick hair and bright blue eyes; both had a sense of the ridiculous which sent them into peals of laughter at the funny aspects of life.

One sunny morning things came to a crisis. The two boys were stepping along the street with caution. The thick trees overhead were just coming into full leaf. The scene was peaceful, but Alex was not deceived by its outward aspects.

"You watch the left, Joe," he told the younger boy. "I'll keep my eye on the right."

The words had hardly left his mouth when a crowd of colored boys came darting out of a narrow alley. Before they knew it the two boys were surrounded. "Don't fight," Alex advised. "There are too many of them, and they're too big; we wouldn't have a chance."

"O.K."

The two boys stood quietly together while the leader of the gang examined them with hard-jawed interest.

"Smart white boys," he said, hoping to provoke an incident. Alex and Joe were silent.

"Throw down your books," he commanded. Again the two boys complied.

"Now turn out your pockets!"

The brothers made no move to execute this command. They were seized at once and their pockets were rifled: lunch money, pencils, marbles—everything was taken. A window went up across the street and a bald head popped out of it. "Hey, you— what are you doing to those white boys? I've called the police!" The colored phalanx scattered in every direction.

Joe and Alex picked up their books. "We can't tell Dad about this," Alex said. "After all, we're men, not sissies. We can beat this ourselves."

On the remainder of the way to school the two boys talked of future strategy. "We can beat them if we stick together," Alex promised Joe. "We'll strap our books to our belts. Then if we see them coming we'll run. When they least expect it we can turn on them. Then we'll give them the one two, run again, and repeat."

A few mornings later they were again set upon. Both boys took to their heels and then, at a word from Alex, turned on the first of their pursuers. Alex threw a right to the jaw of a boy bigger than himself, and sent him reeling. Joe tangled with a smaller pursuer and had a boy's satisfaction in giving him a bloody nose.

The running fight lasted for nine blocks, and the two arrived at school somewhat the worse for wear, but breathless and triumphant. They brushed their clothes, washed their marked faces, and combed their hair in the dark lavatory.

"Well, we've still got our lunch money," Joe said.

"Yeah, and I don't think they will bother us for some time."

"But we'll have to tell Papa."

"Yes, we will, all right. There's a tear in your jacket and a cut over my eye." He felt the place with careful fingers.

That night they told Papa. They felt quite sure he would understand. So he did. "Fighting, fighting!" he said with a half-smile on his face. "It doesn't make sense." He stopped his rocking chair and admonished the two boys with a lifted finger. "As long as you don't start it, it's all right. But this is America, a free country. A man has got to stand up for his rights or he won't have them long. Fighting I don't like. There is a saying among our people: 'If I am not for myself, who will be for me? Yet if I am for myself only, what am I?" The two boys went to bed well satisfied with themselves.

The incident was unimportant, but on the meditative Alex it made a lasting imprint.

Self-reliance was a good thing and it was fine to have rights, but why couldn't people live with each other in peace and quiet?

Why were minor groups penalized? Why should they fight among themselves? Why must they fight at all?

Alex Goode's self-reliance developed in many charming ways. There was the time when his dad and mother were away from home one week in summer. Alex was left in charge of Joe, Moe, and Birdie (that was their pet name for Agatha, the little sister they all loved so much).

"We'll clean house," Alex said on Monday morning after the breakfast dishes were stacked in the cupboard. All four carried blankets to the lines at the back of the house, opened the windows, shook rugs and curtains. Alex put two pails of water on the stove and prepared to mop the linoleum in the kitchen and halls.

How it happened he was never sure, but in a moment the corner of the kitchen where the trash baskets were gathered was afire. A ribbon of flame was running up along the curtains over the sink. "Quick," Alex shouted to Joe. "Get Moe and Birdie out of the house." With a wild yell of terror Joe complied. The children were all screaming now, and the neighbors were running into the yard.

When the firemen arrived they found Alex in the kitchen. His eyebrows and lashes were singed, his face was smudged with black. He had a wet blanket in his hands and the fire was nearly out.

Self-reliance, too, demanded other efforts. Nothing would do but that Alex must take a paper route. He had several routes over the years and served his customers on a battered old bicycle bought with his first earnings.

He was not always a successful businessman. Something in him made it impossible for him to insist when people like Mrs.

Peters said, "My husband hasn't been paid and there isn't a penny in the house."

Hearing such stories, Alex would wait and wait again for his money. Sometimes his customers moved away and left no address.

"Yes," his father recalls with a chuckle, "Alex always tried, even when I had to pay the difference."

Alex was the best boxer and the best runner in the neighborhood, but he also stood at the top of his classes, and in every spare moment he had a book in his hand. "How can I know if I don't find out for myself?" he always answered if he was teased for being a bookworm. "The teacher got smart from reading books, and so will I." The pinochle game went on without him, and the noisiest merriment of three lively children failed to shatter the hard core of his concentration.

Two things could always be depended upon to catch his attention: a mathematical problem, and the account of some new wonder in the world of mechanics.

Noting this trend in his son, Rabbi Goode saw something almost prophetic in his words the day Alex was born. That serious, intent young figure under the shaded light—he would perhaps build bridges or even a skyscraper. It was something to be an engineer in this restless country where everything was outmoded in ten years. His first born! The rabbi's hands were always particularly tender on the head of his oldest son when he invoked the new year's blessing upon his children:

"May the God of our fathers bless you. May He who guided us unto this day be an honor to our family. May He who has protected us from all evil make you a blessing to Israel, and all mankind. Amen."

Racial and religious customs, and the close unity of his family, at times brought Alex a sense of extreme isolation. At school he studied the Declaration of Independence and the Constitution. They were collections of glorious phrases, but they were dimmed somewhat by his encounters with reality. There were boys at school who swore at him and called him "Jew boy". They sneered at his *kosher* food, made taunting rhymes on his race. Did that mean he was never to have the full sense of belonging in this land which spoke so well of freedom? There was a flavor of sadness in the ideas that brewed in his mind at the beginning of his teens.

Of a sudden his doubts vanished away. They were bringing the Unknown Soldier home for burial. He was truly unknown, and the whole nation was turning itself upside down to do him honor. President Harding would be at the ceremony, and the Cabinet. General Pershing and his staff. Foch, President Wilson, Premier Briand of France. While Papa read the news aloud each evening he did not see how deeply Alex was touched.

On the morning of the burial—Armistice Day, November 11, 1921—Alex said nothing to the family, not even to Joseph.

He stole away in silence, with only a glance at his battered bike leaning against the shed. Like the pilgrims of old who went to the temple and the shrines that they loved, he was determined to go on foot to Arlington. The autumn weather was heavy after the recent rains. Trees and shrubs were nearing the end of their particolored fall miracle. The silvery mists in the valley had a tinge of hazy blue.

Alex plodded along the road. It was much farther than he had thought, but he finally reached the gates of the cemetery. He flung himself down to rest on the thick grass and breathed in the smell of the living earth. Around him, ranks of white tombstones, all inscribed with loving care. How little space the dead require. Ambassadors, cabinet ministers, generals, humble privates.

The gentle slopes of the cemetery were crowded with the living, swarming in and out among the graves like colonies of ants. Some bent to read the names inscribed on the rain-bleached stones, some chattered, some walked in subdued groups.

Alex went up the slope toward the perfect circle of the glittering Greek amphitheater, garlanded with immortelles and laurel.

The crowd thickened, the amphitheater filled with notables, the cortege came at last, stepping slowly to the muffled music of Chopin's Funeral March and insistent drums. Slowly the soldiers, the sailors, the marines, in their shining uniforms, marched to honor their unknown comrade.

The long narrow box was blanketed with flowers. All the nations had sent wreaths—kings and commoners. And a grateful people had enlarged that tribute with the choicest flowers of the land: California, Kansas, Illinois, Pennsylvania and New York— it was a floral roll call of the states.

The flaunting phrases and the aspiring sentiments "Garlanded by love. . . . prayers of our people. . . . lasting era of peace"— were blurred in Alex's mind. A new music was taking shape in his brain.

"When lilacs last in the dooryard bloom'd,
    And the great star early droop'd in the western sky in the night,
    I mourn'd, and yet shall mourn with ever-returning spring."

They had read the poem in class. Alex had been impressed with it, had learned the opening strophes of the elegy on the death of Lincoln.

This was it again. Men had come out to honor man, to honor

themselves. That wasted figure under the flowers—was it Jew or Gentile? White, black, red, or yellow? No one knew. But on this day men honored mankind without race or creed or color. The ideals of the Declaration and the Constitution were alive, quickening. Their light shone still, though some had not comprehended it.

The crack of the triple salvo of rifles echoed from the low hills. Then a descending melody of high bugle notes, falling like the sad gesture of an arm, not in resignation but in a sign of peace. The great guns at Fort Myer began their slow, their measured boom.

The notables departed, but the crowd stayed on. Alex wandered to the broad veranda of the Lee House. Before him to the north spread out the order of the city; from the gigantic finger of the obelisk cutting the sky to the dome of the Capitol the design was clear and splendid. It belonged to him. Never again would he feel the old, hard loneliness. Others might fail the light; he would try to carry it.

From his eminence Alex also noted the long road home. It looked so short, but he knew he would be dog tired before he reached his house.

For a time Alex forgot the ceremony at Arlington in the rush of his joyful years at Eastern High School, a new shining building; to enter it every day was a pure pleasure for the boy. The school day began with the raising of the flag on the great flagpole at the front. "Liberty and Justice for all . . ." The words were a promise. Then the babble of voices, the scuffing of feet on the marble staircase, the clash of locker doors in the wide bricked halls and, suddenly, the clang of the bells and silence. Math, French, Latin, English, history, and biology—exciting things to learn in an atmosphere of quiet and order. Fraternities, parties, Sam Brian, and a close circle of new friends.

There were sobering influences, too; among them, *bar-mitzvah* made the strongest impression on Alex. Ever since he was six years old he had worked hard to master his Hebrew. In six years the strange flamelike letters were set upon his mind like a seal. He was letter perfect in the concluding verses of the *Sedrah* and had learned to chant selections from the Prophets in his uneven soprano.

To Alex the Sabbath following his thirteenth birthday seemed interminably slow in coming. He counted the days, but his mind continued to race the calendar to their conclusion.

Never had the Sabbath table looked fairer. The silver candlesticks gleamed among the flowers on the white cloth. Another table near by held Alex's gifts; from the midst of them shone the *tefillin* and the man-sized *tallith* with its striped borders and long fringes.

There were happy tears in his mother's eyes when she bent to light the candles and stood erect to ask the blessing. All the faces of Alex's loved ones were bright upon him, brighter than the dancing flames of the candles. There was sorrow in their hearts tonight to see the tenderness of the past melt into the responsibility of a man's future. He was so sturdy there in his new suit, so conscious of the day's meaning.

They were all proud of him next morning. When his turn came, Alex walked to the lectern in the sanctuary with confidence and acquitted himself like a man.

"You have done well, my son," Rabbi Goode said when they

[83]

had arrived home after the ceremony. "I was proud of you. We were all proud."

"Thank you, Papa. Now I *am* a man, but I don't feel any different." He looked down at his hand on which the new gold ring sparkled.

But in time Alex found that he did feel different. On the Sabbath, now, he went to the synagogue with the men. He wore his prayer shawl with the dignity of an elder, and he knew on these mornings that his childhood was behind him.

All aspects of high school fascinated Alex. His studies and reading opened a thousand new paths into living. He could see in a dim fashion how much there was to learn, how much to read, but every new gain was like coming into a splendid room from which halls opened on vistas in the far distance. The prospects excited him.

There was temporary excitement, too, in the gym classes: boxing and wrestling, and in free time games of tennis played on the courts near the river.

And the new talent he discovered—a flair for oratory. It started in class with debates. Alex was surprised at his success. It astounded the boy that people could be so easily swayed by reason and facts. He discovered too, after a time, that his success depended upon the artful use of his voice. The tones of the human voice—they summed up the most intense and inward memories of the ear. The whole past of sound was in them: funeral solemnities, the sob of remorse, the arrows of repartee and satire, the lighthearted occasions when men had been carried away on the wings of laughter.

Alex practiced oratory incessantly. The family twitted him on his long sessions before the mirror and the pompous passages he declaimed from *Macbeth* and *Hamlet*. It was good-natured chaffing. Alex retorted in kind, for he could see they were proud of his triumphs, prouder, perhaps, than he was. Their voices teased him, but their eyes and faces told another story.

All these minor things were dimmed before a new radiance— the casual discovery of Theresa Flax. They lived in the same section of Washington, only a few blocks apart. Sometimes on their way to school they happened to catch a glimpse of each other. To Theresa, Alex was the boy with the bright blue eyes, and Alex probably remembered her as the girl with the enchanting smile. It was in French class that the ice thawed beween them. Sometimes when Alex forgot his French book the teacher suggested that Alex look on with his neighbor. It always happened that the neighbor was Theresa. It was a charming introduction to a further serious estimation of each other. Underneath their banter they were both beyond average in their maturity. Theresa had high ideals of love and life. The more she saw Alex, the more he seemed to measure up to her standards. Alex was less slow in coming to a conclusion. His friend Sam Brian said later that Alex told him early in his acquaintance with Theresa: "That's the girl I'm going to marry."

Alex was a shy boy and he went about his conviction shyly. His first date was asked and denied. Alex was disposed to be hurt at first, but the next day in class Theresa explained her reason for not being able to go out with him, and said she was sorry it had not worked out. Alex felt better after that. The door was still open. In between the demands of his new evening job, ushering at the Capitol Theatre, Alex found time to teach Theresa the joys of tennis. The boy disciplined his own fast style of play to the pace of his pupil. They found themselves at home with each other.

Sometimes Theresa stood on the side lines at the track watching Alex sprint among the swift runners. With the other students she cheered herself hoarse at his victories.

She also guided him in his first attempts to dance. Like all extreme individualists, Alex did not learn without some effort and pain. Under the floating crepe-paper streamers in the gym he struggled with rhythm. He was determined to learn the art of dancing and he did. "Alex was always on his toes," Theresa explains, "and in those first dancing days he was on mine too."

Still Theresa knew it was none of these things which intensified her interest in Alex. It was the deepness of his mind which drew her. True, he was a delightful boy in looks and manners. He played hero to those less talented in athletics. But these things, she knew, were the superficialities of living. It was thought and interior discipline which made the true man.

Theresa was quick in thought and one of the most popular girls in the school. Under her light manner she was also deeper than the average student. Her observations had taught her to respect mind—and the stories of her own people hammered the idea home with finality. In the Talmudic legends and modern Hebrew and Yiddish romances the "beautiful maiden always lost her heart", not to a knight in shining armor but to a "student with his nose in a book."

Alex was much more alive than that conception. His blue eyes had a thousand changeful moods, and his muscles followed hers in the rhythms of the dance. His mind was a still more beautiful instrument, and whether in thought or word Theresa found him well worth knowing.

For his part, Alex discovered in Theresa his ideal of womanhood. She was modest and unassuming, but in actual discussion she showed a competence he did not find elsewhere among the girls he knew. Compared with Theresa they were shallow. They had no font of sympathy in them which welled up into magnificence in a world of plans and ideals. They were quick to appreciate the physical; the world of thought made them uneasy.

Before they knew it the last halcyon year of high school was upon them. It began as the two-garage year of 1929. For Alex it was a year of triumph. He received a medal for his success at track, and won first place in the oratorical contest in which he had placed second the year before. He and Theresa were savoring the last delights of unfettered youth and adolescence. Their senses were sharp that spring. Big phrases were on ardent lips— "Beyond the Alps lies Italy" "The American Dream"—woven into class poems and addresses.

This underlying feeling added an almost hysterical gaiety to those last days in Eastern High. There were pictures to be taken for *Punch and Judy,* the school yearbook, fraternity affairs, parties, suppers, and dances. The halls bubbled with young laughter, and even the clumsy and plain took on beauty and grace in the excitement and the nostalgic atmosphere.

There were also decisions to be made. Alex had always vaguely thought of being an engineer. His family and friends had too. His last year in high school had somewhat dimmed that idea. Alex's flair for oratory and his deep interest in books had shown him that his talents indicated another direction than he had supposed. He and Theresa talked and talked about it.

Through Theresa, and his father's friend Rabbi Rosenbloom, Alex had met Rabbi Simon, one of the leaders of the Reformed rabbinate. The Washington Hebrew Congregation was the largest and most influential in the Capital. Rabbi Simon himself was a man of books and scholarship, but such interests had accentuated his love of humanity. Above all he was quick to detect the coming leaders of his people. Rabbi Simon brought home to Alex that his talents appeared to point in the direction of scholarship and the rabbinate.

Alex was quick to see the possibilities. Machines and engineering feats had seemed bright goals in his childhood, but were these things different from the childish desire to be a fireman or an engineer? His interests had shifted in the interim. They were centered in human affairs, in men and women and their development. It was obvious that he was cut out to be either a teacher or a rabbi.

The University of Cincinnati and Hebrew Union College offered the fullest opportunity to satisfy either or both ambitions, but the course called for eight years of study and a tremendous outlay of cash. However idealistic he might be, however heavy with dreams, he was brought up short before this hurdle.

Rabbi Simon's wife solved this part of the problem. In her own right Carrie Simon is a great and gracious woman; almost single handed she revived the idea of the temple sisterhood in the reformed temples. She and the sisterhood of the Washington Hebrew Congregation came forward to provide Alex with a basic scholarship which would insure his education. More than this would be necessary to provide the extras, but Alex was sure he could find a job—any job—and eventually tutoring, which would provide the necessary funds to close the gap. That assurance brought him to graduation night with a delirious joy.

It was no wonder that Alex, that night, stumbled in his eagerness to go forward to receive his diploma and athletic awards. For him life beckoned; his imagination was running toward his destiny with ill-concealed impatience and wide-open arms.

For some years Alex had looked forward to joining the National Guard and he had put that idea into execution in the summer of his third year in high school. The first summer, camp life had seemed difficult. Long marches and extended drill did not come easy to a boy—even a young athlete. But, as the hot days wore on, Alex learned to love the life. The rough comradeship, the jokes, and the set pattern of existence had a kind of soothing quality. His muscles hardened; he was able to show his mettle in the field of sports. He added to his fame as a runner and was able to demonstrate the skill in cookery which he had acquired from watching and helping his mother.

After graduation Alex was thoughtful and happy in his second year at guard camp. Sometimes he went through the grounds before reveille sounded. Out beyond the neat rows of dew-drenched tents, slack and discouraged in the faint light, the beaded grass and the trees shone against the pink horizon. His own bright future was beckoning.

But would Theresa wait for him? Everyone loved her, though not, Alex felt, as he did. How could he expect a woman like her to wait out the years until he could support her? She was the only woman for him.

Bronzed and smiling, he came home from his second camp. Deep tan accented the blue of his eyes. Alex recounted his experience to Theresa, laughing at the edge of the tennis court while they waited their turn to play, and her dark eyes smiled back at him. He managed to insinuate something of his thoughts of their future into everything he said.

Always Theresa answered: "It is too soon to decide these things. Besides, who but a fool would make plans in this time of growing depression?" Their minds were busy with the black news in the papers. They all had firsthand experience of the lines of hungry men waiting for a handout in the parks and free soup kitchens. There was gloom on the land, indecision in the Capital.

Yes, Theresa was right, Alex thought. It would be a hard time for all of them. Perhaps, too, his scholarship would be withdrawn if things got worse. "Still," Alex told Theresa, "it is a time for trust in God and trust in the nation."

His first years at Hebrew Union College and the University of Cincinnati were clouded with the despair about him. Alex began cautiously. He hitch-hiked to Cincinnati in order to save his money. The journey was not without difficulty. Men did strange things under the impulse of fear an hunger, and people had become cautious about picking up strangers along the roads.

Alex's care for his funds was justified upon his arrival in Cincinnati. There, too, he found the same frightening gloom he had left in Washington. It was hard for a man to get a job, and for a boy of his age employment seemed out of the question. He watched every penny and counted out his dwindling hoard with reluctance.

The new life he found packed with interests. Languages—now he could see, were sparks which flew between mind and mind. By their tenuous threads the wisdom of the past came down to him. He began to see the relations between groups of kindred words. It thrilled him to discover the beginnings of language in words that described the Deity. It seemed to him that man had remained almost inarticulate until he began to reason about God.

Hebrew Union College was a delight to Alex. The dormitory was comfortable (a gift of the temple sisterhoods), the gym boasted all the latest equipment, and the library was magnificent —the third largest Jewish library in the world. Books, pamphlets, manuscripts, incunabula—the place was a gold mine to one who loved learning. In the Bernheim building at the front of the new library there was a fascinating collection of Jewish art and ceremonial centered about the famous Kirschstein art collection of Berlin, which Julius Rosenwald, Ben Selling, and other loyal friends of the college had presented to the trustees in 1921. There were prints, oil paintings, *Hanukkah* lamps, spice boxes, medallions, coins, and illuminated marriage contracts.

The grounds of the college were beautifully landscaped and it was only a short distance from them to the University of Cincinnati.

With the enthusiasm of a young beagle Alex explored everything. He also found it easy and cheap recreation to saunter about like a tourist. He went to Fountain Square, the center of the city. The noise of the water dripping from the outstretched hands of the colossal female figure made a tinkling noise which was soothing to the mind and the emotions. Up and down the terraces and hills Alex trudged. He went to see the Rockwell Potteries and often spent a meditative Sunday in the Art Museum.

The more Alex pursued learning, the more he came to love history. His interest in this subject stemmed from his own insatiable curiosity. He wanted to know the past in the hope that he might understand his own confused times. Perhaps there were clues in the history of civilization which would help him to see the virtues and defects in the American system. One thing was sure, men went on making silly and stupid mistakes and there must be many lessons in history which would point out methods for avoiding them in the future. History was a palimpsest, but the writers were always men. Surely they must have learned some wisdom from age to age.

The professor of history at Hebrew Union College taught in a wooden fashion. He read his own notes in a monotonous voice, and the past seemed inexpressibly drab as he retailed it in class. Yet Dr. Marcus fascinated Alex; he could hardly be matched by anyone else the boy had ever known.

The manner Dr. Marcus employed in teaching history and the *Talmud* was not what attracted Alex; it was the personality of the man. He was a complete scholar in almost every field. In casual conversation all sorts of recondite knowledge came spilling out of his speech. That glimpse of learning recalled to Alex his high school vision of the great mansions of learning, and life awaiting exploration and mastery. Life took on incredible excitement and fullness in his being able to see the vision and in following it with a humble heart.

Alex was grateful to Dr. Marcus for another reason. In his classes he met Eli Pilchik. Good friends are rarer than ripe scholars. In Eli, Alex found his own devotion to scholarship reflected. They both revered Dr. Marcus and both eventually put themselves under his guidance when they came to write their theses. They talked history incessantly and took long rambles in which they discussed life and literature with amiable heat.

Eli had a particular admiration for his friend because of Alex's common touch. In dealing with men Eli was content to get their ideas first and deal with the *possibles* of conduct; Alex had a quality of uncompromising idealism which made him in a sense intolerant of anything less than the ideal.

Alex also came out to the dances in the school gym, but these, too, held little interest for him. He was always comparing every girl he saw with Theresa and he was content to stand on the side lines watching the dancers, lost in the dreams of his future.

A discussion seemed to be the only thing which took him completely out of himself. A misstatement aroused his immediate and complete interest, and called forth a characteristic expression: "What are you talking?"

The summer of 1935 was an important one for Alex. He spent it in and around the Capital city. By this time the fog of despair and inertia had lifted from Washington and the nation. Under the leadership of Franklin D. Roosevelt the city filled with bright young men who believed in America. Optimism was the order of the day.

Theresa had a good job in the office of Ben Cohen and "Tommy the Cork," two of Roosevelt's chief advisers. With the prize money from college essay contests and the fruits of his tutoring and social service Alex had bought a decrepit Oldsmobile, affectionately called "Betsy." He was helping at the temple in Arlington on the high holy days and was busy with camp and the National Guard. Yet Betsy was often seen standing before the door of Theresa's house on fine summer evenings.

Now Alex had confidence in himself. He felt it was time he and Theresa were married. So many times he had asked her, but each time she said: "Wait a little." First they were too young; then it was the depression. Now those times of gloom and indecision were past. He was within two years of the rabbinate and was growing in power as a writer. Still Theresa insisted she must not stand in Alex's way. "I want you to be a great man. You will be, I'm sure."

"Not without you I won't."

Finally Theresa was convinced. Alex was bursting with joy. He looked at the engagement picture in the paper a thousand times. It was Theresa indeed, the way he knew her best. The dark, sparkling eyes, the turn of the head, the very provocative cut of the hair.

"Daughter of Nathan and Rose Flax," the paper said, "niece of Al Jolson." These details might be important to the world, but not to Alex. She was *his* Theresa, and that was all that mattered. He had waited for her almost as long as Abraham had waited for Sarah. His singleness of purpose had won her at last.

Long hours were spent in discussing their future. The idea of a big social wedding was displeasing to both of them. They seriously discussed an elopement. Wouldn't it be fun to surprise everyone without all the fuss and feathers which went with a formal wedding? The idea tantalized them and they gave it up with considerable reluctance. There were sound reasons against it. Alex was soon to be ordained. A certain stability and dignity were expected of him. He owed so much in love to those who had helped him: the sisterhood of the temple, their families, Theresa's mother, who had been like another mother to him in these years at school, urging him to write, calling him for bridge or supper. No, they couldn't let their families down, or their public, either.

Showers and parties went forward. And their plans too. Theresa would remain in Washington with her family; Alex would return to Hebrew Union College. The "new" car would make it possible for them to see each other often, or fairly often.

October 7, 1935. The wedding day had finally arrived—it was only a few hours after the *Yom Kippur* services were over. Alex and Theresa had kept the ceremony utterly simple. On this point their families had given way, not without argument. In her bridal dress Theresa walked down the staircase alone and into the living room where Alex and the family awaited her. Her grandfather, Rabbi Yoelson, read the ancient Hebrew service in his deep voice. They gave their consent and tasted the cup of wine, first Theresa and then Alex. The groom's hands shook with excitement and the depth of his feeling.

Theresa's grandfather addressed the bride and groom, telling them of their responsibilities. Theresa was too excited to remember much of his sermon, but she was sure it resembled one which

Alex later delivered for a wedding in his own temple in York, Pennsylvania:

"This is more than a mere occasion. All Jewish marriages bear the term *Kiddushin,* denoting sanctification. It is so called because the husband and wife dedicate themselves to the creation of a sanctuary—Jewish home. The ideal of marriage is far more exalted than that which seems to prevail among the so-called sophisticates today. Judaism traditionally has a high regard for the sanctity of marriage. It advises the groom: 'Honor thy wife for thereby you enrich yourself. A man should be careful about the honor due his wife because no blessing is experienced in his house except on her account.' A Jewish proverb urges: 'If your wife is short, bend down and whisper to her'—meaning no man should think himself too superior to consult his wife about business. Together they have the important task of building a lasting home. This is far from an easy matter. It requires constant consideration for each other, tact, mutual restraint, and many other qualities without which the sanctuary is destroyed. Our rabbis have said: 'A man's home is his wife,' and one rabbi never called his wife 'wife,' but always referred to her as his 'home.' This thought requires emphasis today because many have forgotten that wife and home go together. Without a true home, sanctified by love and ideals, no marriage can survive."

In a moment the women were kissing Theresa in a rain of tears and good wishes. The men shook Alex's hand. After the wedding supper Theresa threw her wedding bouquet to her dear sister Ethel. The day finished with a noisy departure in Betsy. An old shoe and some rattling cans had been tied to the rear bumper. The inevitable "Just-Married" sign was wired to the back of the car. With a lurch Alex and Theresa were off to Virginia Beach for a four-day honeymoon.

The last two years at Hebrew Union College washed over Alex like a flood of deep content. His mind was opening out now, deepening too. He had written his first serious essay, *A History of Jewish Philanthropy in America Until the Civil War*. This work, submitted for the Rosenberg-Schottenfels Memorial Prize, offered by his college, showed Alex's mastery of a competent logical style. It also demonstrated the basic direction of his interests in the social scene. Economics had got hold of him. Some of Alex's new wisdom in this field went into another long essay, *A History of Jewish Economic Life from 1830-1860*. In his view of things there was no genuine difference between these past times and the times in which he himself lived. Social solidarity and kindness, these were the two keystones of economic health in any age. These, and these alone, could moderate selfishness and give some equality to opportunity.

Continual thought on the subject moved Alex to form his own plan for the re-employment of idle men. No one particularly noticed the "Goode Plan." Alex was not known, or able to speak with authority, but he felt his plan had solid merit to commend it. In brief, the plan contained the following points:

1. New legislation which would compel employers to increase their men at work by 10 or 20 per cent.

2. No men to be laid off.

3. No wages to be cut.

4. Any employer who was able to prove a loss resulting from putting the new men to work would be compensated by the Government.

5. Any undisposable surplus piled up by the extra labor would be purchased by the Government.

6. Every business participating in this plan would be required to file a business report before hiring any new men under the plan.

Alex intended his scheme to be stimulant to business in times of depression; it would become inoperative in healthy business cycles. In effect, the plan was not radically different from that eventually adopted to aid the farmers.

Most important for Alex, at this time, was the thesis he had to present in partial fulfillment of the requirement for his rabbinical degree. Scholarship, especially that of the German type, likes to be ponderous. It must take itself seriously. Alex chose his subject with care. The very title was ponderous: *A Critical Analysis of the Book of Yosippon as Compared to Josephus and Other Sources with a Discussion of the Literary Problem of Its Composition and Style.* Alex pored over his sources in Cincinnati and at the Library of Congress. His stacks of note cards mounted. Other students labored over their writing—but not Alex. His mind was a precise instrument and he could turn it to a precise problem with ease. His earlier written works, his reading and endless thinking, had opened up paths through consciousness and unconsciousness to the great reservoir of the subconscious. The written word had become for him like the flower to the plant.

Between his tutoring jobs, waiting on tables, the serious work he did for B'nai B'rith, and the long hours these tasks entailed, Alex spent considerable time perfecting his speaking techniques under the nominal guidance of Cora Kahn, the elocution teacher at his college. He did not achieve that humorous turn of phrase which distinguishes the master of irony; he did not have the racy ease of the born raconteur, yet he did arrive at a style which was his own: easy, logical, alive with ideas.

In between times Alex managed to write two other prize essays which demonstrated his scholarship, long study, and subtlety of thought. One of these works was a careful study of *The Exilarchate in Babylon During the Talmudic Period*; the other was a work of equal length which traced the history of the Passover through the mazes of the *Talmud*.

His thesis for the rabbinate was accepted, and Alex passed his examinations with great credit. The day of ordination was at hand.

Theresa came down with her family. They were staying near Cincinnati with relatives. His father and Joseph were there too. All his loved ones had come to share in the triumph which Alex felt was more theirs than his own. It was love that had made all his happiness come true. Theresa was in and out of the school grounds, snapping pictures of him in his new formal dress—swallowtailed coat and striped trousers—but he was the same old Alex of the shining eyes and the quips.

On the Sabbath of ordination his family was in the chapel, watching and praying. At the solemn moment Alex stepped up to the platform. The sacred doors were folded back from the glory of the Ark.

Dr. Morgenstern, the seminary president, placed his hands on Alex's head and intoned the Hebrew phrases which have been used in ordination since A.D. 200. *Yora Yora. Yadin Yadin.* "He may teach, he may teach—He may judge, he may judge." Now he was a teacher and a judge in Israel. The solemn determination of his lifted face was a good augury for his success.

The new honor called for festivity and celebration with his

family and friends. No one loved such occasions better than Alex, but a serious part of him was anxious to put his knowledge to the test at once. All those years of study must be put to work, the sooner the better. If he had acquired any genuine wisdom, it would flower in act. This was not like those fortunate periods of history—the age of Pericles or the reign of Victoria—in which a man of thought could expect to win his spurs through the favor of the oligarchy. It was an age of the revolt of the masses. The man of quick thought and pungent phrase had to descend into the hurly-burly and by practical demonstration show his ability to inspire, lead, and succeed.

At the back of his mind Alex had a sense of haste—perhaps it was a sense of fate. One current moved him forward to the crown of the education for which he had laid such a solid foundation in thought, speech, and the written word. His work at Hebrew Union College and the University of Cincinnati had been good; he wanted the Ph.D. to complete those early labors.

Alex kept his dreams for the ear of Theresa alone. Their first honeymoon had been too short, Alex always maintained. Now, after ordination, they set off for Niagara Falls in battered Betsy. A second honeymoon they called it.

Hand in hand, like two laughing children, they gaped at the falls, went down into the Cave of the Winds, rode the little steamer to the edge of the cataract. But it was the gorge below the falls which really fascinated them, gave them a sense of power such as they had never experienced before.

They didn't know it but they looked more like a newly married couple than the newly married couples did. By slow stages they pushed Betsy down through upstate New York. They loved the country round about Lake George, and the blue lake itself with its clusters of pine-dark islands.

They followed the skyline drive from Elmira to Baltimore. Coming through York, Pennsylvania, Alex said jokingly to Theresa: "Take a good look, you might live here someday."

Back in Washington the oppressive heat of summer was upon them. There were bridge parties and dinners—family parties. All their friends wanted to entertain the new rabbi and Theresa. In their spare time, little as it was, Alex corresponded with everyone who could help him to secure a pulpit. Several offers came in. One in particular interested Alex: the Reformed temple in Topeka, Kansas, needed an assistant rabbi. It was providential that this arrangement could not be worked out to the satisfaction of Alex and Rabbi Wolsey. Alex was reluctant to leave the East and all hope of obtaining his doctorate.

Through his friends, Ephraim Rosensweig and Mrs. Friedman, word came to Alex that Temple Beth Israel in York, Pennsylvania, was searching for a new rabbi. The congregation was small, but what an opportunity it offered! It was only forty miles to Johns Hopkins University, in Baltimore, and Alex would be in complete charge. "Oh, Theresa," he told her, "I must get this place. I must. I must. It means everything to me."

His friends worked hard to obtain Alex a hearing. He was given an opportunity to preach before the congregation of the temple.

He chose for his title "The Sweetest Song." In his sermon Alex demonstrated with clarity the necessity of two things in man: faith and love. It was love of God which begot love of man; it was faith in God which protected love and kept it aspiring in the service of humanity. Without faith in God and love of Him social betterment and social progress are the barren words of Fascism and Communism. Alex ransacked the wisdom of the great rabbis to prove his point, and the language he em-

ployed to clothe his thought was both logical and lyrical. His concluding sentences were the inmost thoughts of his own heart:

"God in His love for us is our friend and comrade who will
aid us in the titanic task of bringing the universe to perfection.
Our love of Him and His creatures smooths the path upward.
For love is not the victory, but the effort; not the goal, but the
struggle; not the result, but the mighty research of the soul and
heart of man."

The personality of the speaker and his unusual sermon won
the congregation. Alex was accepted within a week.

He had delivered his trial sermon on July 16, 1937. Eight days
later his friend Ephraim Rosensweig wrote Alex a cordial letter
of congratulation. There was a significant paragraph in it:

"If ever the moment comes when you wonder whether 'pull'
was not really the greatest factor, when you doubt your ability
or capacity, bear in mind that Mrs. Friedman and I only obtained
a hearing for you—it was yourself who won the pulpit.

"Good luck then, you two! I would hazard the guess that your
rabbinate would be a joint venture; your individual success a
dual achievement."

The letter touched Alex. The gracious shifting of emphasis
to himself, the mention of Theresa. "What a man he is," Alex
told her. "I owe him more than I can ever repay. It is kind of
him to give me the credit, but I am what others have helped
me to be." He looked at Theresa and kissed her. "And that last
sentence is the most true of all and the best in the whole letter."

They were both over their ears in work those first months in
York. They settled in at the Elm Terrace Apartments. The

living-room windows looked over the hills. Theresa set Alex's desk there that he might have the maximum of light.

She bustled about arranging her new home. There was furniture to be bought and arranged, endless typing for Alex, her Sunday-school classes to be started, people to meet. There were also little suppers and hurried lunches for new friends and acquaintances. The barest warning over the telephone was enough—Theresa always came through. With a few bowls of flowers and her genius for effacing herself, visitors went away from Elm Terrace with a feeling of having encountered themselves in public for the first time.

Alex himself fairly bounded with energy. The warmth of existence intoxicated him. He made himself acquainted everywhere; joined the Elks and the Rotary, took out a membership in the Y.M.C.A. He injected life into the *Temple Bulletin,* spoke for any organization at the drop of a hat.

On the surface York seemed a sleepy town, but its outward face of neat red brick houses with white stoops along shady streets was deceptive. Underneath this surface, civic life was throbbing. The citizens all knew one another and there was friendliness in every co-operative achievement. York was proud of itself and it bustled about its pride.

The city fascinated Alex. It seemed like a mass of clay waiting for the hands of a potter, or the strong, shaping fingers of the sculptor. It was naïve, innocent, good; it waited but inspiration and action to declare itself a masterpiece.

Temple Beth Israel was a small Reformed congregation. The temple itself was almost inconspicuous. The modest brick towers, the stained-glass window of David playing on the harp, the tiny porch with small Romanesque pillars, hardly obtruded on the quiet of narrow Beaver Street. Alex was never a mere apostle of bigger and better elephants. "Dynamos are not necessarily big," he always said. Beth Israel should be such a dynamo if he had anything to say about it. It wasn't big, it wasn't rich, but he would make it hum.

Mere activity never fed Alex. He felt the need of mind in everything; he had to grow inside if he was to furnish power for the dynamo. For Alex the great choice for men was between a world of thought or a world without it. In his mind the choice was obvious. A world without thought was dark; it showed the nihilism of the void. But a world with thought was like the first days of the world—every living thing throbbed under the newly-created light.

In keeping with this belief, Alex set about making his convictions reality. Betsy had lost her top in a recent windstorm. Alex immediately purchased a new car which he could ill afford.

One morning Alex drove to Baltimore. In the city he resolutely pointed the new car toward Johns Hopkins. A jubilant Alex bounded in on Theresa at Elm Terrace late in the afternoon.

"I've done it! I've done it! Registered at Hopkins two days a week. The Ph.D.'s in the bag." Theresa wondered how he would find time to do all this work with the tasks he had set himself in York. It didn't seem possible.

The friendliness of York responded to Alex and Theresa. Alex was soon a favored figure at the Y.M.C.A. His card was thickly marked with X's which demonstrated his constant attendance.

Alex thought he had found the secret which made him understand people. Their very aggressiveness was a kind of nervous shield which they employed to screen themselves from the darts and envies of the world. Behind it they were only too often fearful or shy. They waited for the olive branch of a phrase or the flash of an emotion which would tempt them to drop their shield and become one with the others they envied.

Alex had the happy faculty of being able to attune himself to any mood. People enchanted him—their reluctances, and their changes of mood and pace stimulated him to perpetual challenge.

On free mornings Alex worked on his sermons and conferences and the *Temple Bulletin*. Two days a week he dashed off to the university in Baltimore with his books. The "perennial schoolboy," he called himself. Neither mental nor physical activity really tired him.

At the end of the day he would run into the Y. for a quick game of squash or handball with Dr. Langstone, or one of his other friends. En route to the locker room Alex never failed to stick his head into the office of the director, Jason Snyder, for a moment's chat. Jason's ease of manner and his quick efficiency in running many varied programs taught Alex how to make the most of any effort without tiring himself.

At the Y. Alex particularly liked Doc Bleeker, the athletic director. Doc, though his hair was graying, was a splendid example of physical fitness. His good humor stimulated Alex to wit. He impressed his new friends with his good fellowship, and they recalled him later as having had no hint of stiffness, or false clerical front. In coming out of the pool Alex always dashed into the locker room and donned his Homburg before he put on a stitch of clothes. It made them all laugh to watch him clowning, and they recalled with pleasure his quick response to the variations of locker-room humor.

Once in a basketball game with several ministers (without a referee) one of the players called a foul on another player. Alex came loping down the floor. "Don't be so damn pious," he called. There was a loud laugh and a loosening of clerical faces and cummerbunds. The game proceeded in the same casual and un-official manner in which it had started.

At this time Alex began to show an active interest in scouting and the inter-faith movement. This last activity was no mere hobby with him, no wordage which meant lip service to ideals. He knew, as perhaps no other among them, the need of charity and tolerance which meant what it said. He was able to demon-strate this in a notable manner during his first winter in York.

One wild February night there was a tremendous screech of the fire sirens. The noise went on and on. The whole town turned out. When the last embers guttered, St. Paul's Evangelical Lutheran Church was a drift of smoking ashes.

Without a moment's thought Alex offered his own synagogue to the hard-hit congregation. He said they were quite welcome to use it. He meant exactly what he said. The offer was refused with the most cordial thanks of the congregation.

Men, whether of his own faith or outside it, were not always up to Alex's standards in the field of human relationships. His own mind was logical and sincere and he went straight to the point in stating his ideals and what he thought were the proper responses to them. Sometimes his forthright statements brought about the opposite of what he had intended. They merely shocked the people they were expected to convince. The shock set faces against him and led to conduct which could not be rationalized. If Alex was discouraged by these rebuffs, he did not complain or let his failures sour him.

He had an abounding pity for men. Not the pity of conde-scension, but that born of understanding. People debated things with heat and even intolerance. Yet what lent wings to words and insight to thought was their common humanity. The real essence of their greatness of equality was summed up in the fact that they were men. Such things stimulated Alex to further thought. He was lost in his dreams sometimes. Then he would awake from them in the narrow streets of York. The reality and squalor about him ate into the young man's imaginations and hopes.

It was clear that people had to be more than convinced if they were to act. It was necessary to prepare them to receive ideas. They had to be made receptive before they could be carried along toward better things. That was a wasteful system, Alex saw. Education was the only hope, and it was a process which had to begin very young. All creeds and races had their ideals and pieties, which were in themselves a stimulus to love of one another and love of men. But in fact and action such ideals too often evaporated. Old prejudices and tags of hatred came into operation. People themselves didn't realize how or why they were swept away into actions or reactions. There was a code in human relations, Alex was sure, which could be taught with the same ease as a code of manners. The place to begin was in the schools. The children could be taught something of manners in human relations: that creed or color or race were not bars to common action which was in the interest of all, yet guaranteed for all the specific excellences they prized and followed.

At this time Alex found himself repeating over and over again in his mind a passage from the prophet Malachi: "Have we not all one father? hath not one God created us? why do we deal treacherously every man against his brother, by profaning the covenant of our fathers."

In such fashion God had spoken to the Jews, but His words were only too frequently ignored in action among them, in the same way that Christ's words of love and brotherhood were among the Gentiles. Children could and should be taught these things in the schools, but how to begin?

The answer to his query seemed almost providential, for at this time Alex met Victoria Lyles, superintendent of primary education for the schools of York. She had for a long time mulled over the very ideas which were agitating the mind of Alex. They were not in conversation five minutes before they discovered that they saw eye to eye. This young clergyman, Miss Lyles saw, was full of genuine radiance and compassion. His language was dignified and elegant, but his spirit was gay and lighthearted, overflowing with optimism. Between the two of them they began a practical plan of education in human relations. They established a library of books on the subject. Alex and his coworker were not foolish enough to fancy they could accomplish miracles overnight, and they made haste slowly.

They worked on two levels: youth and maturity. There had been segregation and bias in the night schools, and the same thing was glaringly evident on some of the school boards. Both vices, in time, were almost completely eradicated. In the schools, bulletins were designed to give complete information on the varied races and creeds. The children studied one another's backgrounds, and when they knew the truth unvarnished, they saw they had nothing to fear. Prejudices evaporated in the light of truth, fancies went down before facts. The work had so far progressed that Alex could be quoted in the *York Dispatch* two years after coming to the city of York:

"Where there is intolerance and bigotry in our midst let us take steps to enlighten the uninformed. The best cure against religious hatred is information. Let us know one another better and thus learn to appreciate the good inherent in every man."

These steps were not enough to satisfy Alex. He worked in the ministerial association and the inter-faith movement toward the same end. When the Feast of Pentecost came round (the harvest festival), Alex said to the teachers: "Why don't you all come down and see how we celebrate the feast?" Down they went to Beth Israel, on Beaver Street. The temple was bright with sheaves of grain, fruit, and flowers. Alex with some pride showed them his library. Catholics, Protestants, Negroes, and Chinese, they trooped through the rooms of the little temple. It was a mind-widening and heart-warming experience.

"Laughter is the best medicine for prejudice," Alex always said. "If we can laugh at ourselves, we can be sure of our sanity and justice." That, too, had to be put into practice.

Miss Lyles recalls a charming dinner party sponsored by Alex at the Hotel Yorktown. The diners were four in number: Miss Lyles, the president of a nearby college, Rabbi Goode, and Father Howarth. Over the coffee Father Howarth told jokes on the Catholics, Miss Lyles about schoolteachers, Rabbi Goode about Jews, and the college president exposed the foibles of his own profession. Having laughed with one another, they found themselves able to comprehend the serious sides of their varying natures. It was a lesson in co-operation, but a far deeper one in humility.

"There can be no doubt of it," Victoria Lyles asserts, "Rabbi Goode educated the whole town of York in social relations, and the plan he and I started has now gone through the whole state of Pennsylvania. Rabbi Goode's influence directly or indirectly touches every primary school and high school in the state. In this regard at least his life goes on in a wider sense among the young men and women of our nation, and it is only a question of time until his name will be remembered everywhere."

Nineteen thirty-nine was a banner year for Alex. With the permission of the board at Johns Hopkins, he had been permitted to work three days a week instead of the two he had first planned. Between his multiplying activities at the Elks (he was their chaplain), the Rotary, and the Y., in addition to his other jobs, Alex had brought his thesis close to completion. A full list of his clubs and activities makes his achievement almost fantastic, for in addition to those clubs and organizations already noted, Alex was active in scout work, and he served his own people in countless ways: the Jewish Organized Charities, the United Jewish Appeal, United Jewish Council, B'nai B'rith, and the Board of the Jewish Community Center. Moreover, he was a member of the Social Service Club and the University Club.

Alex was an active member, not a mere joiner. He believed in being a participator in all the movements of his time and city. He gave radio talks and addressed meetings at any time and place. Yet he did it all in such a relaxed and joyous fashion that people were glad to hear his words and renew themselves at the font of his idealism.

The frightful persecution of the Jews in Germany made Alex all the more aggressive. It was no time to relax. The coming world crisis called for both courage and forthright speech. The papers labeled the first years a "phony war," but to the Jews in Germany it was anything but phony. They were herded into frightful camps and began their march to the furnaces. No humane person could watch the spectacle without being moved to protest or action.

Alex did not spare himself. He was always going, giving, driving himself forward with a sense of destiny and a strange inner compulsion for haste.

In the midst of so many worries and activities Alex needed

encouragement. This Providence provided in the birth of his child. In preparation for the growth of his family Alex went looking for a new apartment. He found one at 582 West Market Street—a two-bedroom affair. It had a commodious living room with a large bow window and a long yard at the rear bordered with beds of flowers. It was a "restricted" neighborhood, with all that word implies of anti-American snobbery and prejudice of race and color.

The warm friendliness of Alex melted the barriers away. He and Theresa got to know everyone in the neighborhood. They were shining examples of the American way and of that depth of loving kindness without which all religious profession is sound and fury.

Theresa had been expecting for some time. On a snowy Sunday morning in December she remained at home. Alex set out for Sunday-school classes in which work Theresa normally helped her husband. She managed to do the housework in slow stages. She rested in the afternoon.

In the early evening Alex brought her a tray: he was not full of bland and useless encouragement, but his eyes spoke. He rigged up the radio in the bedroom so that Theresa could hear Jack Benny's program. "But don't laugh too hard," Alex said.

In the middle of the program Theresa sat up. "This is it," she told Alex. He bundled her into her fur coat and drove her to the hospital.

The Goode tradition of first sons went glimmering. The baby was a girl, as Alex and Theresa had hoped. They had already selected her name, Rosalie. It combined the name of Theresa's mother, Rose Lea, into one word.

Alex was a proud father. The second or third day he insisted on snapping a picture of mother and child, which he showed to everyone who would listen to his glowing comments on them. He also prepared a letter which went into the *Temple Bulletin:*

"The congregation is happy to welcome into its fellowship its latest member, Miss Rosalie Goode, daughter of Rabbi and Mrs. A. D. Goode. Miss Goode arrived in York early Monday morning and although spending the holiday at the York hospital will reside thereafter at 582 West Market Street.

"Our latest member had an uneventful trip on the way to York. When asked her opinion of the York community, Miss Goode promptly replied in a manner that left no doubt as to her enthusiastic approval. In fact, she was at a loss for words to express her approval, but it is expected that within the next two years the words will come more readily. This bulletin has no recent picture of Miss Goode available; otherwise it would have printed her likeness. Instead, the following description should suffice. Miss Goode is a slender brunette of moderate proportions, weighing about seven and a half pounds. She does not believe in the current fad of dieting, but has the old-fashioned idea that a good appetite is worth developing.

"When interviewed, Miss Goode was enjoying a real Pennsylvania Dutch breakfast. So we say: 'Welcome to you, Miss Rosalie Goode.' Miss Goode may be visited beginning Saturday. She stated that 'any friend of her parents is a friend of hers, and she is anticipating meeting them all.'"

In the early months of 1940 Alex worked endless hours. There were examinations to be passed at Hopkins and the last revision of his thesis to be pondered and polished. Alex had chosen his title with care: *The Jewish Exilarchate During the Arabic Period 640–1258.* The work traced Jewish freedom and independence under Arab rule during a period and in a sector on which little light had been thrown. It was a distinct contribution. The 202 pages of text were heavily documented with 122 pages of appendices and eleven pages of bibliography. The thesis was dedicated to Theresa and Rosalie.

Alex received his doctor's degree in the Lyric Theatre. Theresa was there watching. That coveted gown with its black velvet bands conferred upon Alex the stamp of approval of the learned world. He looked much younger than his twenty-eight years, Theresa thought, watching him assume the bright hood. But Alex himself was proud, not for his sake but for Theresa and the baby. If the world said he was worthy of honor, it did no more than confirm the light in their eyes.

Once again Alex had no sense of having arrived. From this point, roads led in every direction, and he wanted to explore them all. He launched himself with abandon into the new existence. Articles from his pen began to appear with more regularity in *B'nai B'rith National Jewish Monthly*. He turned to book reviewing and became a popular Chautauqua speaker with his talk on "Judaism and the Democratic Ideal."

With the end of the "phony" phase of the war Alex was shocked at the sudden fury which broke upon the world. He watched with mounting anguish the debacle in Holland and Belgium, the swift development of the tragedy in France—the divided leadership, the apathy and cynicism, the triumph of selfishness.

Alex threw himself into the movement to provide bundles for Britain. He was at the radio for every speech Churchill made, and marked with approval each pronouncement of Roosevelt which declared our determination to stand with the British. He intensified his work for the Red Cross, too, and wrote a flashing book review or two.

He was so busy that Theresa sometimes expected him to come home tired and wrung out—yet he never did. Always he would dash into the Y. before supper. A brisk game of handball and a quick swim in the pool kept him in prime physical condition. While Theresa prepared the evening meal she could watch Alex on the blanket spread on the lush grass of the yard at the back of the house. He tickled Rosalie and tossed her up in his arms. To watch him, one would think he was on vacation without a care in the world.

Inwardly he was seething with desires. His brother Joseph had already joined the growing American Army. Alex was convinced that he, too, should be in the midst of things. It was only a question of time until the United States would be involved in the war. He wanted to be in the heart of the struggle where the young men of the nation were forming the future.

Prudence and worldly wisdom were all against taking such a step. A tremendous sum of money had been spent on his education. Dare Alex chance the possibility of throwing all his advantages away, and losing the fruit of those years of study and labor? There were innumerable tasks at home that were crying aloud for scholars and devoted men of complete education. These were some of the thoughts in the mind of Alex: these were perhaps what people called "prudent thoughts." To Alex, prudence meant something different. It was "the courage of the brave" which spoke out truth when other men trifled with it; which leaped into decisive action while other men hung back.

Alex was full of his own plans. In January, 1941, he applied for a chaplaincy in the Navy. There was no immediate vacancy, he was informed. His disappointment was keen. He intensified his work in the camps near York, studied Braille late at night, and in every spare moment was bent at his desk working on a new book. The idea of it had grown out of his Chautauqua work, his experiences with men and organizations of the most varied sort. These contacts demonstrated the need for some sort of school text on the democratic ideal and its history. In Alex's mind the idea of the book and its conclusion were summed up neatly in his own words:

"The coming world is to be a community ruled in the spirit of democracy. What has seemed like civilization up to this point is but a crude effort compared to the era that lies just before us. The new world, held together by bonds of religious idealism, is the goal of democracy through the ages. Toward this new world the cavalcade of democracy marches on, heralding the century of humanity."

Alex's method was simple: he traced the roots of democracy to their first beginnings in the Scriptures, and followed the stubborn development of these ideas down through its varied changes and survivals, through the ages and philosophers, then traced its resurgence in modern times clothed with new force and vigor. His style was logical and direct, but it showed some lack of the color necessary for the writing of the text he desired to produce. Alex saw this himself. He worked to simplify his sentences and he combed the encyclopedias and magazines for pictures which would illustrate his meaning and the force of his ideas.

All these things took a secondary place in his mind after the black Sunday of Pearl Harbor. Alex felt that blow like a personal thing. He was choking with indignation and more determined than ever to become a chaplain. He applied for a post in the Army, and when events moved too slowly he brought pressure to bear.

The period of waiting was a time of torture to him. He would call Theresa from his office in the temple: "No letter came here this morning. They didn't send it home, did they?"

"No, there's nothing here."

"How can they be so slow?" Alex fumed in the evening. "I can't understand it. That's no way to fight a war. I was in the National Guard for seven years. That ought to count for something and entitle me to some sort of priority."

At last the formal notification came. It was a day of delight for Alex. There were a thousand arrangements to be made: someone had to be found to take his place; endless farewells; things to be stored; business arrangements to be made. . . .

Alex went to Washington. Joseph met him in the crowded station. It seemed like old times. They slapped each other on the back, and lived over the old days in the joys of conversation.

In the afternoon Alex went downtown to buy his summer pinks, and the Tablets of the Law for his collar. Joseph pinned them on. A group of young officers being outfitted seemed interested in this strange insignia. "What on earth is that?" one of them asked Alex.

"These are the Tablets of the Law, the insignia of the Jewish chaplains," Alex explained. His voice was quiet, but Joseph noted his pride, the quick swelling motion of his chest, the quick lift of his shoulders.

Alex was happy to be selected for the Chaplains' School at Harvard. The course was a practical one: map reading, first aid, protection against chemical warfare, a small amount of law. The days were full, and the men were all quartered together in one building. This was the best part of the course, Alex thought. Presbyterians, Dutch Reformed, Jews, Methodists, Catholics, Baptists, they were all thrown into close contact—it was a problem in human relations again. Friendships were formed which cut across all doctrinal differences. It was their humanity which was the common denominator, and men were first attracted to one another by human qualities. They learned about one another at firsthand. In these circumstances the most stubborn prejudices had a tendency to evaporate.

Alex particularly liked the sports, the calisthenics, and the small amount of drill. It was like a return to his summers in the National Guard. Some of his colleagues were not so fortunate. They had let themselves grow slack; their feet hurt, and their muscles ached at night. It also gave Alex considerable pleasure to prove on the ranges his ability to handle a rifle or a machine gun.

The month's training went by far too soon. Before he knew it, the little group of chaplains was scattered over the country to the various camps.

Alex was sent to Goldsboro, North Carolina, where he was to be the Jewish chaplain of the Army Air Force base there. The new chaplain was pleased with his new assignment for personal and practical reasons. His father was not far away, in Winston Salem, and the duties at the camp called for every ounce of wisdom and vigor he had.

Rosalie and Theresa came down to join him. At first they lived in the Hotel Goldsboro, but in a short time he found a bungalow which they shared with Cloyd and Mary Goates. They were Mormons, and Alex and Theresa found them charming. Yet in spite of his content Alex was not able to satisfy himself that he was doing everything he could. He wanted active service on an active front. It was well enough to inspire and help to entertain men far from home—they were often lonely and full of complaints; often in trouble, much of it their own making, but the fields of the world where men were dying called to something in Alex which he could not deny.

He wrote Rabbi Bernstein in New York, asking for overseas service: "All I want is a better opportunity to serve at the earliest possible moment." Alex agitated on a higher level in Washington. He wrote to everyone he knew there: friends of his own, or friends of Theresa, people who had known his father. "It is harder work getting into the foreign service than it was to get my Ph.D.," Alex said to his wife. "If they don't say something soon, I'll go to Washington and blow my top. If they'd at least send me some kind of answer, the waiting wouldn't be so hard."

The affirmative reply, when it came, was an order to proceed to Camp Myles Standish at Taunton, Massachusetts, one of the eastern ports of embarcation.

In October, 1942, Alex, Theresa, and Rosalie went to visit Rabbi Goode in Winston-Salem. It was a happy reunion. The baby was three years old now. There were comments on her looks: "Yes, she looks like Alex, but her eyes are brown, almost black, like Theresa's."

"That's my one disappointment," Theresa answered with a laugh.

A kind of solemnity was on them all. They knew Alex would be sent abroad soon. Something about the set of his jaw and a lack of the usual lightheartedness which had been one of his best characteristics, these were the signs their eyes were quick to read. He had rushed the work of his new book and *The*

Cavalcade of Democracy was completed and ready to make the rounds of the publishers.

Alex broke the news to his father, "I'm being sent abroad for battle service, Dad!"

His father said nothing in reply at first. They walked slowly up and down across the path at the back of the yard, talking of many things, sparring to avoid solemnity. At last Alex could bear it no longer. He put his hand on his father's arm. "Dad, I'm likely to be shipped out. It may be soon. Are you surprised?"

His father replied without his usual smile. "Son, two of your names are Elijah and David—outstanding names in our history. One fought to preserve our faith; the other for the honor of our people. You seem to be doing a good work in Goldsboro—you are, I know. Why should you leave that?"

"Surely I don't need to tell you that, Dad! You remember that when they built the temple in Jerusalem everyone brought gifts but the Levites. They were excused because they served the temple. Though we are not of the family of Levi, we are Levites by profession. This is all I can bring as my gift in the cause of my people." He pointed to the *menorah* on his collar.

They walked on a few steps in silence and stopped near the edge of the path. There was a glassed-in hotbed there. Rain from the night before had filled it with water. Alex pointed to the shining pool. "If you will think of that as the well in Bethlehem I think you will understand how I feel. You remember, Father, you told me the story so often when I was a boy—how David, sick with fever, yearned for a drink of cold water from the well of Bethlehem. Some of his men, hearing him speak, fought their way through the Philistine lines. They obtained the water but several men were killed in getting it. When the survivors returned with the water to David, he poured it out on the grass.

'I cannot drink the blood of my people,' he said. That's how I feel." Rabbi Goode said nothing in reply. He gave Alex his blessing.

In November Alex met his coworkers at Taunton. He was happy to see Chaplain Fox again—they had been classmates during their indoctrination training at the Harvard Chaplains' School. They spent some happy hours recalling old friends in the service and the amusing aspects of their first days of Army training. Alex met other chaplains for the first time. Father Leighton, who had been a pal of Rabbi David Eichhorn; the popular Clark Poling; and Father John Washington, whose Irish sense of humor kept him making droll comments on the high brass and life in general.

Alex was touched, too, that York had not forgotten him. He found at Taunton a letter from Jason Snyder enclosing a free membership card to the Y. at York for the duration of the war. Good old Jason, he must certainly have a letter of thanks:

Dear Jason:

Thank you very much for the membership card good for the duration in the Y.M.C.A. It reached me just in time since my new address will be APO 10,440, care of Postmaster, N.Y., N.Y. My duties as chaplain are most interesting and worth while. Our soldiers are more serious-minded than in other wars; they seem to know the high religious purpose for which they are training and fighting and as a result chapel attendance reaches unheard of figures. In my personal contacts with the men it is also apparent that it is a deep religious feeling which underlies their patriotism and idealism.

The folks back home should be proud of their boys in the service and it is not too soon to begin planning for the day when Johnny comes marching home again. In the meantime the homefolks can do nothing better than to write their own kin and friends who are in the service, for a letter from the home town is the greatest aid to morale that any soldier can ask for.

I'll write again from my new station wherever that may be.

Sincerely,

Alex.

Scuttlebutt and secret orders indicated they were all going to Greenland. This was in many ways a tremendous disappointment. Alex had nerved himself to danger and endless activity on a European battle front. Now there was to be substituted for these hopes a post where the number of Jewish boys was very small. He would be unable to use the full scope of his talents.

Alex made several attempts to get his assignment shifted to a larger and more active field. He wrote a number of letters and saw General Arnold, the Chief of Chaplains, without avail. His assignment was Greenland, and that was where he would go.

The winter months wore away. Before he was aware of it Alex was on his last leave with Theresa in New York. A transport was waiting.

In the midst of packing his gear, Alex sat down in the clutter and wrote a farewell note to Theresa:

Darling:

Just a hurried line as I rush my packing. I'll be on my way in an hour or two. I got back yesterday just before the warning. Hard as it was for us to say good-by in New York, at least we could see each other before I left. Don't worry—I'll be coming back much sooner than you think. Take care of yourself and the baby—a kiss for each of you. I'll keep thinking of you. Remember I love you very much.

Alex.

IV

CLARK V. POLING

"Clark, Clark!" He vaguely recognized the cooing sound of his name, but what he was, or the fame of his ancestry, meant nothing to him. His whole tiny being was concentrated on the urge to survive the spasms of coughing, the sense of dreadful constriction.

Gradually the coughing subsided and the baby emerged into

[123]

a world of comfort. Lights, noises, the nap of rugs, the cool touch of polished floors and a sense of well-being overlaid his first impressions of the world. But underneath there was the memory of his first struggle to live.

That his home was in Columbus, Ohio, or that he carried the name of the founder of Christian Endeavor and the name of Poling meant nothing to the child. His wants centered his thoughts firmly in his own world; his cries were a protest against other worlds that went spinning on their own orbits apart from him.

It was not long before this unique world was invaded by something at once his own and yet alien. This was his brother Daniel. The new force was stronger than his own; it could move him and tickle him and pommel him when a toy was at stake. He learned to love this alien, but he also learned to protect his own rights. He gave in or gave battle as circumstances and fluctuating temper moved him.

These experiences were inarticulate—but not for long. Pleasure and power came with his first attempts at speech. "Dada, mama!" and "Da" his brother—he crooned the words over to himself, delighted with the sound of his own voice. Speech was magic. It bent his mother's radiant face over him; it brought rewards of sweets and things that made noise. It caused Dada to beam on him and cultivate his toddling companionship. He began to feel like a leaf on a vine which recognizes in its own life the stem which gives its strength.

Dada especially gave him that sense. The vibrant voice and abounding energy buttressed his own joy in being alive. Light in the sky, budding trees, a new baby sister—all these and a thousand other needles of experience etched his consciousness. "Now I lay me down to sleep." The window outside was still gray. Dada's hand felt warm in his, and his contentment did not cease when his fingers relaxed their hold in sleep.

Brother Dan could compel Clark to do what he wanted. But it was wonderful how speech was a weapon more supple than physical energy. Now, when Clark objected to anything he could argue about it. Dan was the stronger, but he could be outtalked and frequently he was.

Yet, in spite of their differences and quarrels, the two boys fairly shadowed each other. Dan had a sense of generalship which Clark loved and tried to copy. Dan was sturdy and handsome. Dan thought of exciting, even dangerous things to do. Dan set the pace and laid down the rules of the game.

Even on Sunday mornings Dan was not without resources. The atmosphere of church could intimidate Clark. Everyone had Sunday faces that declared and demanded decorous conduct. The little organ led the hearty voices of the congregation, the prayers and the lesson encouraged solemnity. But Daniel would pinch Clark and whisper behind the shadow of the next pew. Mother frowned at the giggling pair over the baby in her arms. The two boys would be quiet for a moment, but things not usually amusing were ludicrous against the solemn background of the place and day.

Daddy could be severe with them when they were really naughty, but in minor things he understood children too well to believe that restless boys were anything but normal. He saw their small derelictions with a clear eye, but his seeing took no edge from his joviality.

Clark's world widened out when the Poling family moved to Auburndale, Massachusetts. After the excitement of the long train ride from Columbus there was the excitement of the new house, standing high above the corner of Hancock Street and

Williston Road. Almost directly across the street was the massive bulk of the Congregational Home for Foreign Missionaries and their families. Its red brick, its slated gables made a touch of color in a street of sedate houses that spoke of discipline and orderly living. To the north, the white steeple of the Congregational Church shot up above the trees.

The new house provided plenty of space for romping boys. Inside the fanlighted hall, the subtle rhythm of the staircase, with its mahogany handrail, called an insistent invitation to sliding. The long living room, divided by pillars and centered on the fireplace, promised evenings of marshmallows, hot dogs, pictures, and games in the light of the fire. And best of all, a continuation of Dad's stories, a world in themselves.

Upstairs, beyond the south room, which the two brothers shared, there was a porch. From it the whole world spread out before them. The land fell away sharply to the south toward the Charles River and rank on rank of oak and chestnut trees. In two young minds, fired with Dad's tales of pioneer life, this wooded stretch was the most exciting part of the new environment. In their imaginations the boys had spotted the menacing feathers of redskins on the warpath. Someday they would trail the redskins, ambush them, win a great victory.

These were the carefree years. Still too young to go to school each morning with Dan, Clark played at home with his sister Mary. He had only to think of a game and she was one with him. She could usually suggest variants and embellishments which spurred Clark to further flights of fancy. Mary had a large collection of paper dolls, and these were woven into the play of ideas as lords and ladies.

Through Mary, Clark also experienced his first case of puppy love. Several doors down the block lived the Edmandses. Clark was at home with them. Their kind thoughts touched in him a childish courtesy and charm beyond his years. But it was their golden-haired daughter Barbara who really caught his fancy.

There were times, however, when she and Mary grew too absorbed in purely feminine concerns—dressing their interminable paper dolls, talking about parties and costumes. Clark knew how to right the balance. Swooping down upon them with a wild yell, he would grab a handful of dolls and pretend to bite off their heads. Sometimes he crammed his mouth with bits of paper, and his realistic cannibalism brought both girls screaming to the defense of their paper family.

When Dan came home in the evening, and on Saturday, too, the play of the children had a more adventuresome cast. Dan had only to say, "I dare you!" and Clark and the smaller children were game to try anything. There were slender birch trees in the yard. The children loved to swing in them. They would climb to the top, then launch themselves into space. It was a wild thrill to go sliding down the slippery branches which broke their leap to the grass.

> He learned all there was
> To learn about not launching out too soon
> And so not carrying the tree away
> Clear to the ground. He always kept his poise
> To the top branches, climbing carefully
> With the same pains you use to fill a cup
> Up to the brim, and even above the brim.
> Then he flung outward, feet first, with a swish,
> Kicking his way down through the air to the ground.*

---

* From *Mountain Interval* by Robert Frost. Copyright, 1916, 1921, by Henry Holt and Company, Inc. Copyright, 1944, by Robert Frost. Used by permission of the publishers.

When this game palled there were more daring things to be tried. The oak trees towered all over the place. Dan, with his superior strength, found it not too difficult to shinny up a trunk by grasping the rudimentary branches along its rough surface. Not to be outdone—though his heart quaked—Clark would find a sapling near the tree from which his brother was shouting taunts. When he had reached what he considered a safe height he would swing over into the oak. There was an exquisite moment of fear in the transfer, a current of pure adventure.

Sometimes the game of "I dare you" brought them to the roof of the Wells' garage. It was high and had a peaked roof. The trick was to shinny up the birch trees and drop to the steep slope of the roof. Then, walking gingerly in their tennis shoes, the two boys and their companions would balance themselves on the very peak of the slope. From windows nearby neighbors watched the ascent with terror. Sometimes Mr. Wells was at home and he would rush out of the house and order the boys to come down at once. He was their father's old friend of Christian Endeavor. Clark and Dan respected him, but even his disapproval of their play couldn't dampen the fascination the garage roof had for them. It drew them with the inescapable magic of forbidden things. They were living according to their standards of the full life. To them the grown-up sense of caution simply did not exist when it meant being quiet or being bored.

The Charles River was just ten minutes from the house. Over the hill, across several yards, then a different world of brush and trees, with paths winding down to the water. Here the river made a great curve. In the shallows, schools of silver minnows winked above the mud; the least agitation sent them flying. Here, too, were the frogs the boys could hear gargling during the warm spring evenings. Frogging was real fun. You sneaked up on two bright eyes in the weeds. The least noise was fatal to a catch. Then, with your cap, you made a great swoop. If you were successful, you had another frog to put in the Mason jar; if you were unsuccessful, you had to endure the jeers of the more fortunate hunters.

The woods near the river offered the boys an ideal spot for building a hut of their own. Like the pioneers of their father's stories they salvaged wood and made themselves a series of shacks where they and their pals could have feasts. Once they were lucky enough to find a piano box. That was the best hut of all—a genuine refuge from grownups, though not quite, unfortunately, beyond their authority. The voice of their mother calling insistingly at suppertime was enough to bring them back to the unreal boundaries of their real home.

In summer and fall Dan and Clark found the water of the river irresistible. They couldn't swim, but this was no deterrent to the spirit of adventure. They waded and splashed in the shallows. About their necks dangled shoes and stockings which had to be kept dry for grown-up eyes. Often they went to Norumbega Park, just a few minutes north of the river bend where the boys and their gang usually played. They would scamper up a slight slope and scoot across the rough surface of the road; its stones were harsh, and in summer burning hot to the tender soles of their feet. The lawns of the park were thick, ideal for wrestling and somersaults. In the park there were ponies that could be hired for a brief ride, and boats moored along the edge of the lawn.

On more than one occasion Clark and Dan found an untended boat. "Mine and thine" ceased to exist. They shoved off into the smooth water with clumsy oars. Providence and luck seemed to be with them. They returned to the shore wet, tired—and undetected.

One autumn day, however, when they had appropriated a boat and launched themselves into the stream, through some mischance the river police detected the two boys and came after them. "Pull, Clark, pull!" Dan ordered. They exerted themselves to slew the boat toward the safety of their usual hideout; it ground on the bank, just two oar-sweeps ahead of their pursuers. The boys grabbed their shoes and leaped onto the oozy bank, where thick underbrush promised a safe getaway.

They had not reckoned with nature. The moment they started up the hill they found the ground thickly strewn with chestnut burrs. Their hearts were heroic, but their bare feet couldn't stand the agony.

With red faces the two boys were lectured by red faces. Their real agony stemmed from the fact of being caught. The lecture was brief and forceful. If it had no lasting effect on the two lads, it at least demonstrated the necessity of caution in the future.

Yes, the "Poling kids" were unpredictable. Their sense of fun and life was keen and lively. When they dragged the dead skunk through the neighborhood and left it on the back porch of neighbor Wells, their aunt punished them and they "paid and paid," as their father tells the story.

One evening the sedate neighbors found the Poling house *en fête*. It stood high above the street corner like the prow of a ship; it couldn't be missed. The Poling children were very definitely at home and indoors. From every window of the house streamers of toilet paper fluttered in the evening breeze. Perhaps it was a regatta at Newport they enacted; perhaps the United States fleet was on a world-wide cruise. Neighbors with a sense of humor chuckled. Those without that saving sense or memories of their own childhood probably muttered: "What will those kids do next?"

But the Poling kids had a tender and serious side to them which only some of their neighbors knew. Their mother was ill, already in that physical decline which ended in her untimely death. Clark was particularly sensitive to people. He loved his mother with a great warm wave of love. The transparency of her hands, and her paling, lovely face filled him with foreboding which he later expressed in a poem written during his later years at Hope College.

LITTLE MOTHER

Here, my mother,
"Pretty Head,"
Is a rose,
A deep dark red.
You are white.

Look, dear Mother,
At the cloud,
It would make
A ghostly shoud,
Soft and white.

Gentle Mother,
May I ask
Why your face
Is like a mask,
Still and white?

Little Mother,
Have you heard
The new song
Of mockingbird?
Why so white?

See, my mother,
 The blue sky
  Where the birds
 Fly silent by.
Oh, you're white!

Dearest Mother,
 Can't you hear,
  Don't you see
 That I am near?
You're so white.

Oh! My mother
 You are dead;
  Lying there
 Upon your bed,
Cold and white!

Mother! Mother!
 Lift your head;
  Rise again
 From your bed,
White, all white.

Gently falling
 Comes the snow;
  All is still,
 The clouds are low,
Cold and white.

Weeping, weeping,
 Soft I tread
  On the snow
 By Mother's bed,
Cold and white.

The spray of forsythia brought to his mother's bedside; the warmth of his greeting when she returned from the sanatorium; the shy child's affections like the brush of a butterfly's wings— all these were delicate testimonials of his love. At night, when bedside prayers recalled the names of those to be remembered, Clark's mind lingered on the name of his mother and poured out a petition on her behalf which no words were adequate to frame.

Clark started school at the Whitney public school near his home. On Sunday, brushed and shining, he and Dan went to Sunday school at the Congregational Church. One of his Sunday-school teachers was Isabelle Eaton, now Mrs. Isabelle Davis, who vividly recalls the impression Clark made on her at the time she taught him.

He was about seven or eight years old then and an individual in every way. He was unpredictable, but he responded to direction with obedience and considerable charm.

There were eight boys in Mrs. Davis' class. Clark seemed on good terms with all of them. "At the beginning of each lesson," Mrs. Davis recalls, "after the superintendent had finished the opening exercises, I allowed the boys five minutes in which to talk about anything that came into their heads—and usually there was plenty. Having been brought up with five brothers, I was able to talk with them on most of the sports about which they wanted to talk. At the end of five minutes nothing was to be talked about but the lesson. Well, one Sunday at the end of the five-minute period I, as usual, said, 'Now we will attend to the lesson'; but before I even had my Bible and *Quarterly* opened before me, Clark burst forth with 'Kaiser Bill went up the hill to take a look at France, Kaiser Bill came down the hill with bullets in his pants.' This in a monotone just as fast as any human tongue could possibly speak. Clark never cracked a smile, but it was there in his eyes and of course the boys, and I, too, had to laugh. I finally had to say to the boys that I thought we had better be quiet or we might be asked to leave, and they were good sports and everything was serene once more. (I can still hear Clark rattling that off as fast as he could.)

"Clark may have been full of mischief but whatever he did had a fresh quality about it. You might reprove him but you had to love him."

During the Sunday-morning service Clark must have been fascinated by the two stained-glass angels which flanked the pulpit. There is something Miltonic about them and their great webbed wings. Clark was at base creative and a poet—perhaps even something of a natural mystic.

His friends the Edmandses appreciated the delicate side of the boy's nature. He was curious, and with his early ability to discuss and argue he gave them many amusing moments. He treated them as if they belonged to his world. On more than one occasion the Edmandses invited Clark and Mary for a visit at Marshfield, where they had a small summer cottage.

With Mary and Barbs Edmands, Clark raced the sands, dabbled in the water, built incredible sand castles and villages set with gardens and flanked with smooth white stones and iridescent shells. Digging, chasing sandpipers along the curve of the beach, by nightfall Clark was so tired from play that he fell asleep, and when he woke in the morning he found himself tucked in snugly on one of the deeply padded settles that flanked the fireplace. He liked to think that angels or some magic means had transported him there from his bed during the night.

The Auburndale days came to an end with the death of Clark's mother. When their father came home from the war, not in the best of health, Clark had been upset. His unhappiness deepened with his mother's death. She had simply wasted away, and her going left a tremendous vacancy in the hearts of her children. She had gone to that "better land," they knew; but what would it be like never to see her again? That thought was a horrible lump in the throat.

From the depths of his own loss Dr. Poling knew only too well what the children were thinking and feeling. It drew his love more strongly about them.

His own family were quick to rally round, and it was decided among them that the children would live with their Poling grandparents and with their lovely young Aunt Mabel who had been for months a mother to them until other arrangements could be made. A change of scene would be better for all of them, once the funeral in Ohio was over.

The year spent with Grandpa and Grandma in Wilkinsburg, Pennsylvania, brimmed with new sights and experiences. Clark developed his critical faculties to such an extent that his father had to rebuke the boy for turning them on his grandfather. He began to devour books at an amazing rate. Adventure stories, poetry, history, everything interested him.

Probably at this time Clark began the formation of his series of inner fantasies which were much like the stories retailed in the *Lone Ranger*. About the world he went mounted on a great white horse doing good deeds. Everyone was impressed by his dashing air and competence. With incredible heroism he rescued those in trouble and helped the less fortunate to a happy life.

These were the signs of his vocation to the ministry—not so much his craving to be a hero, but his sense that people needed his help and depended on the qualities he had been given. There was also a deepening sense of responsibility. Much work was demanded of him at school, and his grandparents expected a more mature pattern of life than his mother had done. His heart was sometimes lonely and he thought often of his mother. A little rhyme from his later school days shows something of his state of mind then:

> Mothers have sung to their little ones
> Since time has flown on its wings.
> Mothers have loved as God does above
> Since the very beginning of things.

The year in Wilkinsburg passed swiftly. That meant moving back to the environs of Boston. A house had been bought in Revere Street. School in a new place, the challenge of new friends for himself and the family. Yet they were all at loose ends so long as they continued to be the family without a mother.

Then a new mother came to them, not a stranger but one they had known all their lives. She had been "aunt" to their youth, and they all loved her quiet, gracious ways. With her and her two little girls their own Poling four suddenly expanded into seven, but their new mother took these complicated affairs into her own competent hands in a way that was an assurance of tranquility and order. The house on Revere Street was sold.

Daddy was at the Marble Collegiate Church, in New York City, and the family lived in a succession of apartments and houses on Long Island and in New York. The moment school was over in June, the Poling family moved out of the city and established themselves at Lake Sunapee, in New Hampshire, for the summer.

Clark was at his best in such an atmosphere. He and his sister Anne Louise, in particular, liked to think of themselves as dis-

coverers. On more than one occasion they explored to its source
a brook which ran into the lake. They named their new kingdom Clarkanne in honor of themselves and in true royal
tradition.

Clark was sent to Oakwood, the famous Quaker school in
Poughkeepsie, at the end of his first year of high school. His first
impression was a happy one. The physical roominess of the place
augured well for breadth of mind; green fields, a great sweep of
woods to the south, trim white buildings scattered about the
grounds.

Clark's first impression of space and peace was borne out on
the level of the spirit also. Casual goodness was the very texture
at Oakwood. There was respect for learning and brilliance, but
simple goodness was enthroned among these qualities as an
equal, if not a superior. It was interesting to Clark to discover
that in this school no code was a mere code. Life wasn't some
kind of game to be played according to outward rules which
concealed one's real feelings and character. Conviction and the
rules had to come from within. Otherwise the surface was no
more than a "whited sepulcher."

Oakwood was an important phase in Clark Poling's formation.
The closest and most enduring friendships of his life were
formed here. He continually returned to Oakwood in later life;
it had a fascination for him not only because of its physical
aspects, but because of the spiritual strength he found there.

On the warm plane of Clark's personal life there were many
friends—particularly "Tubby" Painter. Tubby was easy to live
with. He was strong, excelled in sports, and had a bubbling sense
of fun. Both boys were mad over football; they talked it,
dreamed it, and played it with a seriousness that declared how

strong a hold it had on them. Tubby was a year ahead of Clark in his classes, but on the football field they were equals.

Clark played halfback and was cool and brainy in action. He didn't have Tubby's bulk or brawn, but he made up for these lacks by using his head. This consuming interest in the game of football led to results which were memorable to their school. In the fall of 1928, the Oakwood eleven, coached by Mr. Newlin, played their scheduled games without once being scored upon until the final game with Epiphany Junior College (which was out of their high school class). Their opponents were bigger, but they didn't outmatch Oakwood in strategy. At the end of the game Oakwood was ahead. They had won, but their clean record was gone. Tubby and Clark had tears in their eyes when the last whistle blew. The school was wild with delight at the victory; the two boys felt it was less than perfect.

Long walks and games, shared experiences and confidences, drew Clark and Tubby closer together during their Oakwood years. They visited each other in the vacations and widened their community of interests.

With the advent of spring Clark and Tubby began to look forward to their summer at Long House, which Dr. Poling had recently acquired as a summer place in New Hampshire. The house gave evidence of that loving art which went into home building in pre-Revolutionary days. About it the mountains stood up and shouted like Blake's morning stars.

The boys had pooled their carefully saved money and bought a battered Chevy coupé with a scarred rumble seat. The purchase was secret and the boys determined to make their first journey to the new house without telling anyone of their designs. Their suitcases were tied everywhere on the hood and the remains of the fenders; their pal, Kenny Bromage, was tied in the rumble seat. At last they were off with a chugging and a lurching which would have done credit to a runaway threshing machine.

They coaxed the tired, hot engine up hills and pushed when they had to, and that was often. The moment Tubby was ready to cock his feet up on the dashboard a tire would pop, or the radiator spouted steam like Old Faithful. There were oil leaks and gas leaks. Their T-shirts were stained with dust, sweat, and grease; their faces were haggard from effort and loss of sleep. Kenny, alone of the three, retained something of his schoolboy's neatness.

The trip took two days. The last miles were horrible. Clark asked directions in the town near Long House, but at first no one seemed to know the Polings. For a few miserable moments the unhappy trio wondered if they had come to the wrong place. They looked at one another with near despair, but more inquiries melted New Hampshire caution and put them on the road to Long House.

By mistake they took the old road into the house long after dark. It was full of rock and debris. The tired car trembled and coughed, one of the headlamps was out. At last the black bulk of the house loomed up ahead against the starlit sky. With a loud honking of the horn they were in the yard.

Lights suddenly sprang up in the windows, and the family poured down to meet the travelers. In the midst of the rush of talk both boys were quite willing to concede their mistake in buying the jalopy. One resolution they were sure of—never again.

Days at Long House were not merely days of pleasure and loafing. There was work to be done about the place and roads to be built. Everyone was expected to do his part. The hay had to be put up, there was bread to be kneaded, and wood to be sawed and split. Then there was the Dutch oven, which Mrs. Poling had reconditioned. It was a wood eater, and Clark and Tubby were required to see that everything was ready for baking day. The two boys sweated over their task. Clark was critical of all Dutch ovens; he thought the whole thing more or less of a bore. But when after grace they all sat at table, sometimes as many as twenty-seven of them, he was convinced of the oven's virtue. The beans were unbelievably good and the bread was better than any cake.

Through many summers spent at Long House Clark learned to appreciate and love his new mother. Her goodness, and the interest she had in everything beautiful, called to his mind and heart. Among his papers there remains a little poem, "My Second Mother", in which Clark summed up his boyish love:

> At your feet, my Second Mother,
>   This poor heart of mine I lay;
> And the years will bring no other
>   Dearer than you are today.
>
> For in years of happy living,
>   Since you came to mother me,
> Always have I found you giving
>   Strength and love unstintingly.

Dr. Poling's presence in the small town attracted many famous visitors. The pastor of the Marble Collegiate Church was a personage of note, and Mother Poling was the very essence of hospitality.

Now, on Sunday morning, the little church wakened to expectancy. Famous men ornamented the pulpit. Once every summer was Poling Day. The whole family pitched in to make it something special. When the service was over, all the celebrities trooped out to Long House, to tables loaded with fried chicken and baked ham, with homemade ice cream and fresh berries for dessert.

It wasn't only at Long House that Tubby and Clark built up their memories. For two summers the boys worked on Dr. Campbell's farm, pitching hay, looking after the herd of Guernseys, helping with the milking.

Clark had an engaging way with people but he couldn't boast the same success with horses. The Campbells had two work horses, Molly and Dolly. The horses were devoted to each other, so devoted, in fact, that one horse would not work without the other.

Clark sniffed at this horsy affection. "It's ridiculous," he said, with a boy's wisdom. "Dr. Campbell wants some cultivating done today and I'm going to do it. It's silly taking both horses. I'll take Dolly alone, and believe me, she'll learn to work."

Several hours later Dolly appeared at the barn whinnying with joy at sight of Molly. Clark was nowhere in sight. He appeared later, red and somewhat the worse for wear.

The corner of the field in which Clark had tried to enforce his discipline on the unwilling horse looked as if a cyclone had struck it. Clark dismissed the whole episode airily, but he confided to Tubby that Dolly's grandmother must have been a Missouri mule.

All too soon it was time to return to Oakwood, but Clark and Tubby had endless experiences to recount over chocolate sodas at Smiths' tuckshop during the coming months, and they were both brown and strong, and raring for football.

Oakwood left other than the marks of friendship on Clark's character. Dr. Reagan, the headmaster, admits that Clark did well in his studies but not so well as he might have done had the boy exerted himself. He seemed to have no desire to achieve top marks.

In one field, however, Clark did excel—in English literature. It wasn't his reading alone which made this possible but rather his native gifts. Ruth Craig, one of his English teachers, treasured some of his poems. These demonstrated a considerable talent and facility in verse writing, especially for a boy in only his third year of high school.

One poem gives a deep insight into some of the ideas and emotions which troubled Clark at the time.

> Give me the heart of a rose;
> I would crush it and break it
> And tear it apart;
> I would have all the beauty concealed in its heart.
> But once I found a beautiful rose
> Deep in a garden, lonely and hidden,
> Quietly lifting its heart to the sun,
> Clean with the dew, watched by no one.
> Ah! why is it, though beauty I see,
> I can not make it a part of me?
> The rose I took has withered away;
> The petals are dry, its redness is gray.
> And that which is left is nothing at all
> But an ache and a yearning
> And a cold black wall,
> That took the place of the beauty I saw.
>
> The heart of a rose, its beauty unfolded
> As I tore it apart and saw what was there
> Exposed to the air.
> And the wall that stands where beauty might blossom,
> Shutting me from my hopes and my dreams,

Is part of myself, dwelling within me,
Soiling all beauty, loathsome and mean.
I batter my yearning upon its cold hardness.
Black it remains and repulsive, I trust,
Pulling me downward, destroying my dreaming,
Dragging the things I love in its lust.

I turn from that wall and lift my days yearning
Skyward far up into infinite blueness;
But all that returns is a harsh mocking laughter
Chilling my soul and giving this answer:
" 'Tis useless to call for help from above—
Of stars in their burning, consuming all yearning,
Ignoring all wrong.
So you are a fool to seek after *beauty;*
Roses must die and the wall is of you.
You must submit and leave what you wanted
Dead in your hands. There is nothing to do."

But when I looked at the rose in my hand,
Again it was living, its redness returning.
This then's the answer, an answer within me:
"Beauty is always a part of your yearning."
The sobbing of my bleeding heart
Is quieter, now I know
That if the rose is crimson still
My blood has made it so.

Another tells us something more about Clark. It is a poem written about his mother.

By Mother's knee
In twilight time
I prayed to Thee.

My mother taught me so
In childhood days,
Not long ago.

Strange one above,
From her I learned
Of Your great love.

I pray no longer.
Mother's gone—
And I am stronger.

You needed Mother there
To teach Yourself
My little prayer.

But I am lonesome now
In twilight time.

The peace-loving character of the Quakers undoubtedly touched Clark deeply and remained with him to the very end of his life. The thought that war achieved nothing but destruction became one of his strongest convictions. That, and a man's individual responsibility for making wars, suggested doubts to him even after the time he became a chaplain.

Clark had a sincere interest in student government. Eventually he became president of the student body and a member of the Council. Dr. Reagan says of Clark: "He was one of the outstanding boys in my forty years of teaching experience." In memory of Clark he set down some vignettes of him:

"I have a feeling that both students and teachers would agree that Clark was an unusual personality. He was well liked by both teachers and pupils; he was full of fun and mischievous, but his mischief was not ever vicious and he was always loath to have fun at the expense of other people.

"He was active in school affairs, was a good athlete, a good student, but did not work up to his ability. He was genuinely concerned, both socially and religiously. As president of the student body and as a member of the Council, he would at times find himself in opposition to most members of the faculty. At other times he would oppose the great majority of students. He was kindly and open-minded, but his criticism was keen, specific, and he did not change his mind without real evidence.

"He was an effective president of the student body; a characteristic expression, when he wanted to voice some criticism, was, 'I want to talk to you about something that is none of my business.' Those talks were always precious experiences and his advice was always salutary, for he knew the mind of the student body; and, whether he agreed or not, he could help us see and understand his attitude.

"His life was joyous, unpredictable. One Sunday night screaming girls dragged a laundry basket down the hall; it shot down the stairway almost in front of my office door. When I opened the door, Clark Poling had lifted the cover and was sitting in the laundry basket with head and shoulders exposed. I said: 'Clark Poling, what in the world were you doing?' He answered: '"I have had a ride through the girls' dormitory. I heard lots of noise, but saw nothing. The cover was on all the way."'

"Another instance which I will never forget occurred again on Sunday night when I had gone to the office for the first time after the death of our baby. When I started home, Clark Poling was in the hall waiting for me. He took my arm and without a word walked beside me to our home; he opened the door, said,

'Good night, Mr. Reagan,' and left. It was that keen, sympathetic understanding which endeared him to all of us."

With Clark's graduation at Oakwood he and Tubby decided to enter Hope College, at Holland, Michigan. Dr. Poling was a member of the board at Hope, and he was happy that Clark wanted to go to school there. He thoroughly approved of Tubby Painter, and it seemed logical that Clark and Tubby should be eager to continue at Hope the life of sports and well-balanced activities which had distinguished their friendship at Oakwood.

Tubby had to confess to himself, during the first year at Hope, that Clark's nature was changing. His sympathy with the underdog, his own carefully guarded individuality, his talent for leadership and argument and his interior drifts made Clark intensely moody at times.

All his talents came to a sharp focus at Hope. In one of the early freshman football scrimmages during his second year in college Clark broke his wrist. It was at this time, his father notes, that Clark made up his mind to become a minister. His love of argument seemed to indicate a talent for law, and Dr. Poling was all the more astonished and pleased when Clark confided in him his desire to preach.

For Clark, the two years at Hope held far more than the inner storms of the spirit.

Hope was a deeply religious college. It had kept the Dutch Reformed traditions. Prayer and discipline were the keynotes of the school. The town itself was more than a little tinged with Dutch custom. Clark was surprised by one of these customs the morning of his arrival. Though it was ten-thirty in the morning, everyone seemed to be at breakfast. Workmen sat under the trees with mugs of coffee; the diners and restaurants were crowded; it was the hour for coffee and *kuchen,* an old Dutch custom.

After the febrile activity of the New York area and Long House, Hope seemed a quiet place. But the boys of the college had their own ways of creating excitement. Tubby and Clark lived in a literary society dorm. Fraternities had been forbidden by the college authorities. The literary society provided a ready substitute for young men who thought themselves old enough to run their own affairs.

Clark immediately threw himself into the life of the place. His broken wrist, which ruled him out of sports, was a keen disappointment to him, but he made up for it in diverse ways. Though he was still a sophomore, his writing ability made him eligible for a place on the staff of *The Anchor,* the college paper. He demonstrated his maturity in other ways. There were many charming girls in his own class, but Clark chose to associate himself with a girl from the senior class. He carried her books and took her to dances.

Dancing and poetry became something of a passion with Clark. The Saugatuck, a modern ballroom near the river, was popular with all the young people of the district, whether they were collegians or not. The big-name bands of the country appeared there and Clark, ever fascinated by experience, learned to dance well at the Saugatuck.

Most of the poetry Clark wrote at Hope was love poetry. Late at night, while the dorm snored, Clark was intently composing sonnets and lyric quatrains.

With a boy's idealism he was still bent on helping the under-dog. Chapel was compulsory, discipline was stiff, and Clark was "agin the government." Not that he didn't enjoy chapel. He did. There was perhaps no student of his time who loved the phrases of Scripture as Clark did; the hymns and lessons spoke to his soul with a special meaning. Yet, in spite of this, Clark had minor differences with the school authorities. He wanted learning and religion to appeal to students without compulsion, and he didn't hesitate to say so.

It was a series of minor misunderstandings which eventually led to Clark's determination not to finish his college career at Hope. His speech at the oratorical contest, "While Morpheus Slept," was one of the minor things. Another was the affair of the dormitory.

Clark and five other boys slept in what once had been an operating room in the old hospital. One night Clark came in late—he had been out dancing. It irked him that he still had work to do. He was disgruntled and he gave the door a tremendous bang. In the morning, on rising, the boys found the door had jammed. They shouted and pounded. They yelled and pounded some more, but no one came to help them. They couldn't get out of the room, and the chapel bell was ringing. Clark was anything but nonplused. "Go out the window," he called from his bed. Out the window his roommates went, and down the side of the building, clinging precariously to the jutting bricks. Unfortunately it was at this precise moment that faculty and students filing into chapel observed them. This human-fly act seemed to be a flouting of authority, and of course Clark got the blame.

Such minor things took on exaggerated importance when Clark wrote his editorial against the excessive emphasis on athletics at Hope. It was enough to bring the full weight of academic disapproval upon him. In spite of these minor storms, Clark got through the remainder of his sophomore year with credit. His interests had shifted from athletics and were turned toward poetry and the responsibilities of his coming ministry. Hope no longer suited his changed mentality. He wanted a new atmosphere.

After leaving Hope, Clark spent the last two years of his college course at Rutgers, and then went on to complete his work for the B.D. at Yale Divinity School. His classmates in both places report that his interest centered in people rather than study. He was ready to discuss life and living, he could argue by the hour; then, when exams came, he sat up all night cramming. He might have stood at the head of every class but he had no interest in marks. As a matter of fact, he rather despised them.

His years in New Haven provided innumerable opportunities to demonstrate his talent for people. He wrote reams of lyric poetry, including some excellent sonnets, and he meditated on life; but he showed his real mettle in the eagerness with which he took up the work of his student pastorates at Meriden and New London. In 1937 he cycled through England with Roy McCorkle, and in autumn he returned to his work in New London, Connecticut.

Here in the First Church of Christ, under the leadership of James Romeyn Danforth, he worked quietly and well. Clark's sermons were nothing special, but his effect on the people was memorable, particularly among the middle-aged and the old, the sick and the poor.

Clark had a special sympathy for the old. He saw their loneliness and periodic despairs. His heart went out to them in their black frustrations and the ingratitude which usually seemed to be their lot. In his quiet way the young minister made them see their importance to himself and to God.

On the night of his ordination, which his father has described so graphically in *Your Daddy Didn't Die,* Clark was serene and confident. He knew there was work to be done in the church and he felt that he had already proved his fitness for the tasks before him.

The granting of his degree might be delayed, his studies might not show more than a mediocre promise, but there were already a thousand proofs of the love he had planted in many hearts.

One memento of his success in New Haven always brought tears to Clark's eyes. It was a hooked rug. The woman who made it was old and frail. Into the pattern of the rug she had made—from Clark's enthusiastic description—the pillars and front of Long House. She had caught the feeling of the place, and Clark accepted the offering with the delicacy of his appreciative heart. He took it to Long House, where it still hangs.

Clark was happy in New London. He saw himself growing in the hearts and lives of his people. But he was bursting with new ideas which the small parish he served could not possibly contain.

At this point a kindly fate intervened. His father had dropped into New London for an overnight visit. Such casual meetings were always red-letter days to Clark. Dad was at once a stimulation and a balance. He never saw things on one plane only; he could look at and explain every side of a problem.

In high spirits father and son went out to dinner in a quiet restaurant where their talk would be undisturbed. Clark unfolded his plans to his father. "I'm thinking of visiting the Middle West," he announced casually. "There's a breezy quality out there, and, I believe, a lot of room for me to put some of my ideas into practice. Perhaps I'll find the ideal parish out in the wide-open spaces. I hope so."

His father discussed the idea with Clark. Yes, the Middle West was fine and progressive, but all Clark's roots were in the East. It would be hard for him to tear them up and transplant them in a new soil and a different climate.

The two men were silent and thoughtful as they walked back to Clark's simple room. There, stuck under the door, was the very letter that promised an answer to the problem they had just discussed—a special-delivery letter from Schenectady, New York. It invited Clark to supply the pulpit of the First Reformed Church the following Sunday. Clark's father was jubilant. "This is the answer, Clark. They are looking for a new dominie—a young one. You're the answer, please God."

The dreams and hopes of that night became a sudden-blooming reality. Clark went; he was heard and seen; he conquered.

Schenectady's old church with its strong Netherland style of Gothic architecture vibrated some secret chord in his heart. He was proud of his Dutch ancestry, and this church with its long history called to everything that was aspiring and good in him. Since the time of the French and Indian Wars this plot of ground had been a fountain of the word of God.

By a unanimous vote of the congregation Clark was called to the ministry of the Schenectady First Reformed Church. Clark's family was excited, but not half so excited as the new minister. He took a room in the Y.M.C.A. and plunged into his work.

The congregation came out in force for the formal installation of the new minister. The assembled ministers filed into the church to the "Minster March" from Lohengrin. They took their places in the stalls about the pulpit, the hoods of their academic gowns making splashes of color against the somber gowns and white bands of the Reformed Dutch divines. The grand singing of the congregation: "Saviour, Thy Dying Love," "Faith of Our Fathers," "God of the Prophets, Bless the Prophets' Sons," and "Dear Lord and Father of Mankind" was balanced by the grave words of the office of installation.

There was more than a note of home and all Clark knew and loved. It was his brother Daniel who now charged Clark—he who once had tickled and pinched Clark's baby sides, who had adventured and fought with him, who had loved him these many years. His ringing voice was reading the third chapter of Second Corinthians. Clark's eyes and mind followed that voice to the inspiring climax:

"But we all, with open face beholding as in a glass the glory of the Lord, are changed into the same image from glory to glory, *even* as by the Spirit of the Lord."

This was the same vision Clark had seen from a mountaintop long ago. He recalled how his father had come searching for him, calling his name in terror along the steep slopes. "Dear Dad!" There he was in the pulpit preaching the installation sermon, telling of Christ's formula for the world and living.

How rich Clark felt he was in friends and family, in his brother and father, and in the loving and loved faces of his co-workers: the Rev. Gerard R. Gnade, who presided; his old friend and pastor, James Romeyn Danforth, under whom he had worked for three happy years in New London; his school friends, Howard Conn, George Seibert, and Franklin Hinkamp—these and all the others. They had come to pray with him, to honor him on this night of beginning, of heavy responsibility. Almost before he could count over his wealth of memories the organ was thundering out the "Festal Postlude." He was in the church parlor now. People, his people, were pressing about him, shaking his hand, inundating him with their congratulations and good wishes. In his mind he prayed to be worthy of their love. With a humble heart he promised himself he would do his best.

There were many problems—Clark could see that in the first few days of his ministry. The church was old and historic, but perhaps it had a tendency to live on its pride in the past. That, at base, was a good thing, a very good thing; it reflected tradition —living tradition, not only in stones and memories, but in the very names and faces of some of his congregation who were living history in the flesh. Beekman, Wemple, Ten Eyck, these were the names that had made New York. No, names in history, or in memory only, were not enough to make a parish. Active hearts and souls were needed, and that would be his first task. In his humility Clark didn't even realize how well he was fitted in talent and personality for the solution of his first problem. One thing was clear: church attendance was down to a handful or two handfuls; the Sunday school showed a record of twenty-five children.

Clark set out to meet his congregation in a series of unexpected and casual visits. He didn't want to encounter his people in their formal attire prepared and stiffened for the meeting. Informality was the essence of his strategy.

There are living records of these visits. Among them Arch Wemple, a well-known Schenectady lawyer, loves to tell his story of Clark Poling. One night, during Clark's first days in Schenectady, Mr. Wemple was doing some carpenter work in the basement of his house. He heard a rapid step in the hall abovestairs and went up to investigate. It was Clark.

"I'm Clark Poling, the new minister of the First Reformed Church."

"My name is Wemple."

"Yes, I know."

"Come in, won't you?"

The two men went in to the living room and sat down. Arch

Wemple admitted to himself that he had never before met a minister like this. There was a kind of radiance about him, but there was nothing pious, either in his phrases or ideas. This was a man like himself, but unusual and different. They chatted of sports and religion and social problems. The air was electric with ideas, and the host found himself talking with an interest and completeness he had never known in his life. When Clark stood up with the exclamation, "My goodness! Twelve o'clock! Time all good ministers were in bed—and even bad ones," Arch Wemple couldn't believe they had been talking for hours.

"Oh, I'll come again," Clark said with a smile, even before the invitation was pressed upon him. "You say you've been an indifferent Presbyterian. The Dutch will reform all that." His light laugh punctuated his observation.

Clark's prophecy was fulfilled to the letter. Arch Wemple found himself at church, not occasionally but every Sunday; and his wife and family went with him. It wasn't that Minister Poling was a great preacher. He really wasn't. The mastery of language his father had was not his talent. Perhaps one out of three or four sermons would be really astonishing—unrhetorical, but to the point, getting in between the chinks of complacency and human hypocrisy. It wasn't his speaking, but the man himself that was the magnet.

Clark had a subtle sense of humor too, active in everything he said and did. Once he inserted in the church bulletin an expense account for the building of the First Church in 1803. Among the items listed were several bottles of black rum. The men of the congregation got a great kick out of that.

Clark was a torch, a doer of the word, sensitive, vigorous, manly. People who disliked him or were sharp with him got the same courteous treatment he meted out to old friends. "I have never seen a man so totally without rancor," Mr. Wemple insists. "He made me understand what sort of man Christ was. It would be wrong to say he was a man's man any more than it could be said he was a woman's man or a children's man. He was everyone's man, and I can tell you that strong men wept when they heard he was gone."

Another man, Douw Beekman, has much the same story to tell of the strong impression made on him by the new minister.

At the time Clark Poling came to Schenectady Mr. Beekman had a garage and service station near the church. Clark dropped in one day, and the friendly Mr. Beekman was so impressed with his casual manner, humor, and lack of solemnity that he went to church to find out what this unusual minister was really like. What he found there brought his whole family to an ardent interest in the First Reformed Church.

Beekman, too, bears out Arch Wemple's picture of Clark's personality. "It wasn't what he said or his preaching ability that made us love the man. No shade of malice colored his words or opinions. He was almost naïve in his goodness, and you felt the sweetness of the man in every meeting with him. Clark Poling didn't merely turn the other cheek—he refused to see or recognize the power of evil or hatred. He was so busy making the good dynamic that he had no time for small enmities or jealousies. Most of his congregation lived in the suburbs. Mr. Poling was a true dominie to them, but he had a much wider idea of the role his church should play in the community. The church itself is on the edge of the business district, and Mr. Poling felt it ought to show its power there, and share the burden of the district where it stands. The results were amazing. Lawyers, doctors, bankers—all the public-spirited citizens and men of good will, but without direction, found themselves working in harmony toward good ends. Mr. Poling didn't argue or fret about anything, he simply kept his mind on the ball and refused to be influenced by understandable human rivalries. He was objective in a subjective way, if you know what I mean. You see, he didn't believe in regimentation. He liked people to do what they were doing because they wanted to do it. We all felt we were equals, and he was one of us. You can't imagine what a difference this made in our active participation in church affairs.

"Take the Boys' Club, for example. Mr. Poling picked it up and simply made it hum. He indicated to his congregation that it was a good work. There was no attempt to dragoon the people —everyone was interested, and the church made a heavy donation to carry on the project. The boys' work was tied in firmly with both religion and psychology. The club project was not a surface attempt to fill up boys' lives with activity which would get them off the streets and keep them occupied. Dominie Poling was not of this shallow mentality. He loved the young as he loved the old—as human beings. He didn't condone frailty in a patronizing fashion. He understood it and tried to turn it into higher levels of the spirit. I don't know how well I'm making you understand what I mean, but Minister Poling was a grand human being, and his approaches to all things were so human and understanding that you simply went along with him.

"Clark had a way with the sick! He kept his finger on the pulse of the congregation. The moment you were ill he would casually drop in on you. He didn't overwhelm you with bounding vitality, and he didn't come in to depress you with long, lugubrious prayers. He was there talking to you, absorbing your interest. The first thing you knew he sort of picked you up and you felt better inside, just because he was there. I wasn't much of a church-going man before Mr. Poling came to Schenectady, but he changed all that.

"One of the things I liked best," Mr. Wemple remembers, "was the way he got a group of men together. Before we knew it we were talking social problems and religion. They were fascinating meetings. We learned a lot because even our first timid opinions were given importance, and this eventually led us to take an individual interest in things of the mind and soul. It's interesting to note that this group is still the active core of the First Reformed Church.

"There is another little instance which will give people an insight into Clark Poling's psychology. When the Jews were suffering in Germany, long before the United States got into the war, Mr. Poling didn't go about ranting at their injustice and cruelty. He saw the seeds of the same evil among us. His answer was to ask Rabbi Aaron Wise to the church to address us. The rabbi came several times, and I am firmly convinced we were all better for his coming. Mr. Poling wasn't a say-gooder or a do-gooder; he was just a grand man and he really believed in humanity."

Clark's early success in the new parish was accompanied by the joy which came with his marriage. His courtship, as his father has pictured it, was fast and furious. The woman he chose, Betty Jung, of Philadelphia, was eminently worthy of him.

The marriage, in Philadelphia, was a veritable comedy of errors. The church was too small for the guests. Clark forgot most of the things—flowers for Betty, and the boutonnieres for the ushers. He had to rush out and attend to those matters while the guests were already arriving. The day was sweltering. In the ceremony Clark completely lost his voice, and when he and Betty were ready to go away on their honeymoon they forgot

Betty's clothes. The beautiful bride ended the day with a black eye—not given her by Clark, but acquired in one of the multiple confusions.

After a short honeymoon the newly married couple came to live in Clark's apartment at the Schermerhorn, to which he had moved in preparation for his new life.

Now Clark knew the deep pleasure of shared confidences and plans. His wife was his wife indeed, but she was also a significant personality. Her afternoons at home helped immeasurably in forging the unity of the congregation, her active interest in clubs and Sunday school widened the influence and power of her husband's work. In her own right she was strong, beautiful, good, and very intelligent. People loved her, not because of Clark, but because of herself. Clark was happy to have it that way.

Something of his deep content flows out of the message he wrote for the church bulletin that first Christmas in Schenectady.

"There was a man long ago who was too busy to attend the greatest event of history. Preoccupied by success, for his inn was full, he turned Mary and Joseph away and missed the birth of the world's most precious babe. The innkeeper of Bethlehem would have made room for a king. And had he known the outcome of the starlit night surely he would have received the mother of Jesus. But he could not see possibilities of wonder and beauty in what to him was commonplace. Therefore he is remembered as the nameless man who closed a door.

"Now let us, remembering him, be reminded during the joyous season of Christmas that the choicest gifts of God are not always labeled as such, that His holiest Son was the lowliest child born in a manger. The Wise Men found a king because they sought a king. We may find God in unexpected places. Miracle, wonder, and beauty may be present unnoticed at our feet."

Synthetic stars glittered along Schenectady lawns, fires of welcome were lighted in homecoming faces. In the hymns of the congregation of the First Reformed Church there was a special joy. It had nothing of the synthetic about it. Rather it was the fire of the rekindled heart that warmed them. And the young minister, so at ease in the pulpit, so without pride or ambition for worldly things, retold the tidings of that great joy.

For Clark himself it was a time for counting again his old blessings, his imaginative childhood, his genuine discipline of spirit at Oakwood. He could remember all the gentle hands and the gentle faces which had made him draw out the best in himself. His old friends and his new friends, all that was or had been, were summed up now in the face of his wife and would be kindled to a new radiance in the face of his expected child.

The previous Thanksgiving he had printed in *De Omroeper,* the church bulletin:

"Do you remember the words of the song, 'Count your blessings, name them one by one'? While there are some who would consider this advice naïve, nevertheless it is good-health-giving common sense and all of us should periodically put it in practice. We are too apt to fall into chronic pessimism under the persuasion of the anemic prophets of despair who enumerate all the horrible events of the past decade with gusto and conclude that barbarism is about to destroy our liberal and democratic individualistic civilization. But pessimism itself is more to be feared than the internal misfortune or barbarism that gives it cause.

"Pessimism is 'failure of nerve,' loss of confidence. According to one great historian it was such failure of nerve that from within prepared the Roman Empire for defeat from the bar-

barian hordes of the north. As long as the people of the Roman Empire were confident in their traditions of religion, law, and government, as long as they were energetically looking to the future, no threat from within was serious. The same condition is true today with us: as long as we confidently build on our rich heritage of material achievements, of liberal thought and institutions, we need not fear barbarism or failure. And we certainly are justified in being confident. As we count our blessings one by one we see that as individuals we have unlimited power at our fingertips, greater health expectancy than men have ever had before. We have leisure for pleasure and recreation, and we have opportunities for challenging work.

"Then we look at our nation. Despite trying conditions we are continuing our traditions of freedom and justice and we are wealthy and powerful. Even the difficulties of the past eight years have taught their lessons and we have reason to hope that after a further period of adjustment a net gain will be apparent. The United States will emerge a wealthier nation in material and spiritual possessions.

"Finally, looking at the chaotic world, let us never forget that even in the darkest areas of fear and suggestion, the triumphant spirit of human courage and sacrifice is constant. As always, the most potent force in the world is the force of human spirit, and its faint but steady gleam will eventually illuminate the coming of a 'new heaven and a new earth.'"

Clark was not satisfied that everything possible was being done for the children in the Sunday school. That activity was being run in the traditional manner. Old wine was being poured into the new bottles. The school had already grown from twenty-five to sixty-five; that was something, but not enough. New methods of teaching had come in these last years. None of the new resources of psychology were being used in behalf of children who needed them. His teachers were splendid and devoted to the children; but what was needed was a bridge between the young and the old, between fathers and children. Sunday school alone led to the Sunday-school mentality: one day for God, six days for mammon. How, in one short hour, could children be taught the deepest religious truths? That sort of outlook could only lead to old-fashioned pigeonholing and the building of bulkheads against the spread of religion and truth into every hour of the week and every phase of life.

Clark's old friend, Dr. Ligon, of Union College, seemed to have the answers. His program of character development for children was exactly what the First Reformed Church required if the Sunday school was to be more than a tradition. Clark and Dr. Ligon had been over the ground many times in private. Clark was convinced that the good doctor really had something. This conviction called for action.

Clark talked to his men's group. They, too, were convinced. Early in 1938 a committee was formed to study the plan.

Before summer came, the church had decided to adopt Dr. Ligon's program. The children went off to summer camps or the seashore. But in the fall the character-development program was started in earnest.

The effect of the new system, applied with Clark's individual approach, was electrifying. Clark watched with delight while the Sunday-school membership went up to seventy-five, then to a hundred, and finally to one hundred and twenty-five. The children were really interested at last. That was only one facet of success.

The new system put the chief emphasis on religious training in the home. Parents found themselves faced with new decisions and responsibilities. They were supposed to teach by word and example. On Sunday mornings they were expected to come to church with their children, and Clark held them to that without exception. The family first joined in worship as a unit. Then the children went on to their own concerns while their fathers and mothers remained in church to study and pray.

A happy revolution in church life was gradually achieved. Everyone was active now. There was no more sitting on the sidelines, as if religion was a Sunday-morning amusement, and religion itself a toy. The entire week was a living prayer. It would be a mistake to imagine that Clark rested on his oars or let new interests distract him from his pastoral duty. He went among his people day after day. The sick were cheered with his presence, the boys' club grew and prospered, the civic clubs felt the impulse of Clark's electric personality.

His private life widened into a new splendor with the birth of his son Clark Junior, or "Corky."

But Clark's impulses did not end with the suburbs of Schenectady or the walls of his own home. Like his father, he supported the vigorous policies of Franklin D. Roosevelt, and he censured the cruelties of the evil doctrine that had set Europe ablaze.

His strong attitude in regard to Roosevelt called for some moral courage. The members of his congregation were Republicans and might be expected to share Republican prejudices against the President. Such things made no difference to Clark. He was far too sensitive to invade the political prejudices or private opinions of his flock, but he went his own way with serene conviction. That he had a right to do. So well had he done his work among his people that few questioned the right. Men and women observed him day by day at close range. They prized his selflessness and his lack of personal ambition. They knew that his watchword was service, and without completely analyzing their own thoughts they knew that he had to act according to the inner convictions of his own heart.

Shortly before Corky was born, the Polings had moved from the Schermerhorn apartment to a house not far away on Front Street. It was a big old house more than a hundred years old. Behind it a grassy slope shaded by tall elms ran down to the river.

The new house gave Clark the background of quiet which he loved and which made it possible for him to treat life creatively. People remained his first love. This fascination grew on the young minister. Sometimes on Saturday night, while visiting the sick or friends, he would suddenly jump from his chair, "Goodness! Eleven o'clock and I still must prepare my sermon for tomorrow." He would dash off home, but the next morning he would speak from the pulpit with timeliness and directness.

Sometimes, too, Clark's deep interest in living people caused him to be late for a funeral service or a meeting. Such lapses were not held against him after the first few moments of indignation. Everyone knew how heavily people leaned on him, and almost everyone saw that Clark was trying to be "all things to all men" in the best Christian tradition. There was an inward seeing about the man which always gave evidence that he was a man of God.

On a December afternoon in 1941 the pattern of Clark's life was shattered.

Clark was not a flag waver. He had always been a man of peace, but the Pearl Harbor news filled him with uneasiness. He loved his land, and that land was threatened. That called for action, not alone from others but from him. Ah yes, he was safe: a minister with a child—it would be a long time before he would or could be called up. Common sense seemed to indicate that he was doing a man-sized job where he was. Now, as never before, people would need the strength of his comfort and advice.

Many people have thought of Clark as a simple person. He was not simple in any sense, but enormously complex. First he had to conquer his distaste for war. History and experience, he was sure, proved that wars accomplish nothing. He had expressed his own personal point of view in an issue of *De Omroeper* for July, 1939.

"The most effective way that men have of achieving happiness is by creating personal sanctuaries which cannot be stormed by the forces of adversity, in which things of the mind can be cultivated and in which love, a modicum of physical comfort, and a measure of spiritual tranquillity can be enjoyed. We can build such a sanctuary by returning to the fundamental pleasures of home and family, of good books, and, most important, to the joy of worshiping God. If our happiness is dependent upon these the outside world can tumble about us and we can still have peace. Let us therefore cultivate only those areas of living which bring love, intellectual enrichment, and spiritual contentment. Only as we possess these are we wealthy. Only as we lack these we are poor. With these we are never lost."

All Clark's hopes of spiritual sanctuaries were threatened. Hitler and Tojo were trying to create a world of force. Every man of love was called to stand up and be counted in the coming struggle. How could he bear to withhold himself? He couldn't.

Clark was not the kind of man who scorns advice. He talked about his problems with the men of his parish. The gave him the advice he sought, and he considered it all carefully. Most of the men felt he had a job to do at home. Some were convinced that a man of God denied himself if he became anything but a man of peace.

Somehow Clark was drawn back to Oakwood. There he had first learned that a man must make his own decisions. Conscience and internal conviction must indicate the right answer. He went down to Oakwood for a few days. Old friends were eager to discuss with him every aspect of the great problems of war and peace.

His mind was made up at last. The inner uncertainty hardened into conviction. The young men of his congregation were going to war. They would enter a harsh world, an alien world. How could he talk to them, how would he be able to advise them—if and when they returned—unless he became part of this world? He had to know their problems and share their experiences.

The first conviction led him to believe that he must enlist, not as a clergyman but as a man. Dad would be able to help him settle that problem. His father has set down that part of the story in his own direct fashion.

When Clark announced his decision to enlist, Dr. Poling thought, of course, his son meant the Chaplains' Corps. Clark said no, not that, he was determined to enlist as a soldier.

"What's the matter?" his father asked. "Are you afraid?"

Dr. Poling then proceeded to lay down the cards as he saw them. In World War I the chaplains had sustained the highest mortality rate of all groups involved. If Clark went into the corps he would go in unarmed, in a fashion that suited a man of peace and love. He would share every danger, but it would be his task to strengthen the lonely, support the weak, console the dying. Those were worthy things. Clark got the point. His father was right. He would become a chaplain if that could be arranged.

It was hard for Clark to break the news to his congregation. The step he was about to take seemed to demand his resignation from the First Reformed Church. It was only fair to his people. The people didn't think so. They loved him and wanted him back. It increased his humbleness to think that they refused to consider his resignation. It made him proud, too, that he should be so well loved and appreciated.

The sick, the old, the unhappy, friends and more friends—he saw them all in the last days before he left for his indoctrination training. Schenectady had never looked more inviting than in these last weeks. And everyone poured out for him their choicest wine of love and appreciation.

His first Army days at Hattiesburg, Mississippi, were busy ones. They also had an amusing note in them. For one as widely traveled as Clark he was astonishingly innocent. He didn't smoke or drink, and it rather shocked him to find how much importance men in camp attached to these habits. His astonishment sometimes led his informers to string him along a bit. Some officers said they drank a gallon of whisky a day, and when Clark retailed the news in a letter to one of the men in his congregation they chuckled at his naïveté. It would seem that Clark's shocked attitude at first led men to accentuate their oaths and tough mentality.

The men seemed wicked to the young chaplain, but he gradually worked behind the mask. In these camps men were torn out from their native frames of goodness and normality. The gambling and drinking and lack of restraint were straws erected as a dam against their loneliness. But when the chips were down they were all children at heart. They prayed then, and behind

[166]

the rough surface of their lives Clark could see there was gentle-
ness in them. They helped one another and did more serious
thinking than they would have been willing to admit in public.

After all, he himself was fortunate. Betty was with him, and
Corky too. The frame of his life was still intact. It was but the
glimmer of the old life, but he enjoyed it as the other officers did.
Rented quarters were not home. Always there was a sense of
instability. Tomorrow, what? Danger? Death perhaps. It keyed
one up to a feverish sort of existence.

These snippings of home life the average enlisted personnel
could not afford. Their hunger for home fairly cried out along the
dowdy streets where they lolled against the fronts of buildings.
Their voices were loud in their loneliness. They fought and
drank to make up for the things they missed.

At base they were all human and very dear. They still needed
someone to lean on, to do their thinking for them, to share their
loneliness. The amazing thing wasn't how bad they could be,
but how good they were in spite of the pressures upon them
from all sides: shopkeepers who took them for a ride and abused
them; saloon proprietors who complacently watched them get
drunk and then gave them the boot.

Clark felt he knew them well now, and he did not under-
estimate them or expect too much of them. He still asked for the
best on Sunday, and he was active in everything which could
make the old pieties come alive among the men.

A large part of his heart was still in Schenectady. He wrote
to many of his congregation: Arch Wemple, Douw Beekman,
the Handbridges—the list was large, but it showed how rich he
was. Old friends seemed like an anchor. It was restoring to have
news of that small, stable world—of joys, births, and deaths. At
the beginning of the new church year Clark turned toward his

church. He wanted to tell his congregation how thoroughly he was with them in spirit; how ardently he exhorted them to steadfastness in a world given to war and destruction. On September 8, 1943, Clark sent a telegram to Schenectady which summed up his feeling.

"Betty joins me in sending an affectionate greeting. We will both be thinking of you when church opens Sunday and our prayer will be for our beloved church. I know that you will overcome inconvenience and the petty annoyances which have been thrust upon us by war to make this a great year in the life of the church. We have a fine consistory, ably assisted by Dominie Hinkamp and Dr. and Mrs. Ligon. By the grace of God you will not fail. Never in its long history has the old church been more needed to bring the hope, the comfort, the strength, and above all the love of Christ to the men and women who enter its doors. I have never been more joyfully confident in the healing powers of Christ. Do not be discouraged because of the horror and suffering of this war. Live patiently and sacrificially, with penitence, and remember always that God is not mocked. Many of you have asked questions, and when time permits I will write what Elder Yates calls an Epistle to the Schenectadians, but I could not let the first Sunday pass without this greeting. God bless you."

Clark learned to appreciate more and more the fine undersurface of the enlisted man. His feelings on the subject may well be summed up in a letter he wrote from Camp Shelby, Mississippi, to Arch Wemple in July, 1942.

"Everything about my work here is worth while. I have told some of my friends that not all aspects of the Army are what I wish they were, but from the point of view of my work the worse the situation becomes, the more I am needed. And, Arch, I don't mean that with anything but humility.

"You must live with the people that the Army gives you to live with. The large majority of men and most officers are good fellows, but sometimes you are subject to constant exposure of a low type of man. In my case the enlisted men are far superior in morale and personal habits to the officers.

"Please don't think me harsh. What I have said I say with the understanding (1) that the whole Army has many more fine, clean, decent men than the kind I have met, and (2) the worse the situation the better the opportunity for a chaplain, and (3) even with the worst types, they have some good qualities.

"If anyone tells you the Army is feeding chicken, steak, etc., every day, you tell them that one of your friends at Camp Shelby hasn't met up with such extravagances. They may feed the Air Corps that way, but we get good, substantial, simple food. Another thing, there are no potato peelers except two-legged ones. I eat at an enlisted man's mess with other officers and we get the same food as the men get. Once I started to sit with the men and they, and later the officers, told me I shouldn't. As chaplain I could because that is one of our prerogatives.

"Another time I was pitching horseshoes with the men and I took off my shirt. One enlisted man came up to me quietly (he has an M.A. from Harvard) and said, 'Chaplain, you better put your shirt on. An officer can't be that informal with the men.' "

Clark's chaplaincy had small tendency to make him pompous or stuffy. He wanted to be one with the G.I.'s, but Army tradition and discipline were against it. His heart chafed at his own slow progress, though that was not his fault in any sense.

When orders came transferring Clark to Camp Myles Standish at Taunton, Massachusetts, he was happy at the prospect of active service; but when he discovered that his unit was being shipped to Greenland, the news depressed him. Greenland did not fit his ideal of an active front. To his imagination and his desire for service the field assigned him appeared narrow. A little thinking convinced Clark that his first revulsion had more than a tinge of pride in it. Why should he complain at being sent into the half-darkness of the Arctic night? There the men would need the chaplain much more urgently than they would in any other part of the world-wide front. They would be forced to look for the help of the church in their fight against loneliness.

This conviction was strengthened in Clark's first meeting with some of the other chaplains who were being sent with him: the quiet Fox had worked with an ambulance train in World War I; Alex Goode with his Ph.D. and his interest in social studies; Father Washington with a big future ahead of him in New Jersey. They were good fellows and between them there were almost infinite resources to be used for religion, entertainment, and courage. Greenland would in some ways be a finer test of their stamina than tremendous battles in Africa or Europe.

The final word of their imminent departure came after months of waiting. They were to go aboard the transports soon. The dreariness of Taunton in winter was a proper prelude to a winter and spring in Greenland.

There was a little precious corner of time for a last holiday with Betty and Corky. His son had grown very dear to Clark. Already he noted in the boy the emergence of those qualities which had filled his own childhood with adventure and movement. It was like having the years rolled back for a glimpse of himself or Dan as they had been.

That last embarcation holiday irresistibly drew Clark back to Philadelphia and Schenectady. He came to Schenectady on a

Thursday night. The house on Front Street was like a pair of loving arms. It seemed heavenly with quiet after the bugles and turmoil of Taunton.

There wasn't really time to see everyone in one evening, but Clark did his best. He and Betty kept the taxis busy every minute. First visits were to the sick: Clark, tanned and vibrant, looked good to them. His quick laugh and high spirits were a healing in themselves. Than he hurried about among his friends. Now he knew why he wanted to come back—the very atmosphere called to everything that was creative in him. It pained him to have to depart for Taunton without once more seeing his people in a Sunday service. The feeling prompted him to write a farewell letter which would sum up his emotions more fully than a hasty visit could. Clark wanted to touch all of them in spirit once more before he tore himself away.

"It was good to see many of you last Thursday evening. My only regret is that it wasn't possible to have one Sunday in church before leaving; but I have been very, very fortunate these last months, first in my contacts in the Army and above all in my continued relationship to the church. God has been very good to me and I have not one cause for complaint.

"During the five months that I have been away I have become increasingly aware of the deep attachment I formed for you and our church. I am proud to be your minister and, God willing, I hope to have mutually happy years working with you again. But whatever lies ahead I want you to know that I am grateful for your friendship, and I recall only good as I look back over the four years I was in Schenectady.

"There were times when I have boasted about my friends and 'my' church as I met and tried to impress other chaplains. This may have been a compensation for feeling very green, feeling like the rookie I was. I am sure that many of you have talked in the same way telling about the age and beauty of 'my' church. Now that I am to be away for a long time I am going to remember our beloved church as Christ's Church. And my hopes and prayers will be that as the months and years pass we will be able to make our program of education, service, and worship express the spirit of Christ. Our goal is not to gratify our pride and our human desire, it is to hold high the light of our Saviour in a troubled and confused world.

"Tomorrow I leave for a port of embarkation . . .

"God bless you all.

"Clark V. Poling."

JOHN P. WASHINGTON

Almost every afternoon Mrs. Washington went for a walk with John. When she came down the steps, leading the boy by the hand, curtains would be pulled aside in the neat houses; the whole street watched the progress with absorbed interest. Marion Wirth, the young piano teacher for the neighborhood, peered over the geraniums in her window box. What an angelic child he was! The bright gold hair of the boy was cut in a precise Buster Brown bang. His blue eyes were shining, and a soft flood of pink washed his plum cheeks and the chubby calves of his baby legs. His blue-piped Buster Brown suit was immaculate. Around the corner on Central Avenue they went, toward the arching elms of the park.

Children were a commonplace in Newark, N. J., doubly commonplace on Newark's Twelfth Street, but somehow this child stood out among them. There was an air of primal innocence about him: he reminded them all of the forgotten kingdom of their own childhood—those Eden days which flashed into the memory like intimations of immortality.

The "big guns" lived over in the Oranges—the very name had a hint of the hothouse about it. But Twelfth Street itself was a true microcosm of Newark; Germans, Irish, a sprinkling of Poles, and one colored family, all lived under its young maples in perfect amity. No one was rich, but no one was poor. The houses were small and some of the rooms were dark. Yet many a house boasted a bay window or a more ambitious bow; the back yards were cut by beds of vegetables and borders of bright flowers.

The people on Twelfth Street belonged to that great unadvertised mass of the country—the respectable citizens. They were the kind of people Sinclair Lewis was to satirize a few years later in his best seller *Main Street*. What Lewis overlooked was the truth that they were respectable because they respected themselves.

The Twelfth Streeters were nearly all church-going people. If they quarreled over small differences or let emotions betray them at odd times, these lapses were atoned for in confidences exchanged over the back fence. Sickness or death drew the street together in the bonds of quick sympathy and love. Bowls of soup went to Mrs. Flaherty when she broke her leg; the women prided themselves on their devil's food cakes when there was a christening, a church supper, or a wedding. Then the small boys came out banging on pans and pieces of tin while the windows went up at the racket and grinning faces watched the proceedings. They all shared in the food and the excitement.

Each weekday morning there were two waves of activity on Twelfth Street. The first had to do with the men going off to work. There was a smell of frying bacon, a rush of banging doors. Men ran down the steps with a shouted word of farewell, their neat lunch boxes tucked under their arms; a volley of starting cars made the air throb. Then quiet settled down over the street until the children dashed out of the houses yelling and whistling to one another on their way to school. Except for a hurried lunch hour, the women were free to visit, shop, and enjoy the quiet until school was out in the early evening.

The Washington family was a thorough part of the Twelfth Street atmosphere. Mary Washington was a tower of strength in any emergency, her amiable good sense drawn upon by other women. Frank Washington, with his handsome Irish face and soft Irish accent, was a stable character. His steady job with the "Public Service" marked him among those who lacked his balance or rollicking humor and were in and out of employment.

Frank and his wife loved children. They watched their family multiply with pleasure. At intervals of about two years a new child was born: Mary, Anna, Thomas, Francis, Leo, and Edmund. As these arrived, there was not so much time to spend on John, his daily walks, or his costumes; he took his chances with the rest of the family. But his status as the first born was established by the gilt-framed picture in the living room. It filled the other children with good-natured envy when the examined the exquisite child held there in color by the skill of a photographer.

If anyone got special attention now it was Mary, the second born. She was always pale and delicate. The other children followed the lead of their mother and father in guarding the flicker of life in her thin face.

Mama was a constant like air or water; Papa was romance. Every night the children watched for his return. Supper, waiting on the stove, made their noses tingle. They pressed their childish faces against the windowpane. There was the Buick, at last, stopping before the house. They ran to the door and flowed down the steps. "Have ye been good children now?" he always asked them with a laugh. He kissed them in turn, gathered up an armful of the smallest, and led the rest back to the house.

After supper he told them stories of Ireland. "I remember now," he always started. All the old legends, tales of the leprechauns who lived in the lakes and the forest. Hans Christian Andersen was not to be compared with Papa. In his rich voice the past came alive. Patrick and Finn walked over the living-room carpet. The children saw the far island with its low hills unbelievably green. They wondered why their mother chuckled at times and said, "Now Frank," as if to restrain the exuberance of their father's fancy.

Little John in particular was attracted to his father's wide knowledge and competence. After the first wave of small children had gone to bed he often had fine chats with Dad. John felt it was good to trot out his questions and get straight answers. His father treated him like an equal. The boy relied upon his father's opinions, and even when John was a grown man this attitude remained.

The year Tom was born John Washington started to school at St. Rose's. His mother fussed over him. Mary and Anna were sad but excited. They watched the lively figure of their brother walking down the rainy September street. The day would be empty without him.

To John, this new world of books and pencils was exciting. The school was alive with the restless hum of the bright classrooms with their shining windows on one side. The edges of the blackboards on three walls were bright with mottoes, and there was a red tongue of light dancing before the plaster statue of the Blessed Virgin. The soft voice of Sister imposed respectful order.

The new hymns he learned were a special delight to John:

> Mary, dearest mother,
> From thy heavenly height
> Look on us thy children
> Lost in earth's dark night.

They were like his father's tales of Ireland. There was a luster about them—a mystery too. Why was earth's night called dark, John wondered. Was there not night in heaven too, and how could it *not* be dark?

He asked his father and got an answer, "Even at night in heaven 'tis bright," his father told him, "because Our Lord and all His saints are there. They are brighter than the moon and the sun themselves."

"But how can they sleep, then, Papa?"

"Oh, they have no need of sleep, for they are spirits, lad. When Mary and Our Lord were on earth they slept like we do, but now in heaven they need it no longer."

John couldn't understand that. He was always tired by nine

o'clock. Heaven must be an exciting place, he thought—a place where you never get tired.

There were other things which puzzled the youngster. Some of the boys he met at school swore, and used strange, ugly-sounding words on the playground when Sister was out of earshot. John dutifully reported them to his father. "Those are not nice words," his father told him. "That's language God and His Mother wouldn't like, and boys who talk like that can't be the friends of God or they wouldn't soil their tongues with dirt or swearing. A man talks like a man, not in words that are fit for the animals."

John took the lesson to heart. It fitted in with Sister's words, and the first lesson of the penny Catechism he laboriously learned by rote.

"What is man?"

"Man is a creature composed of body and soul and made to the image and likeness of God."

John also discovered his quick temper. If he made a mistake in class he felt a tide of warmth running up to his hair. He got into a number of fights on the playground. He didn't tell his father about those; a boy had to look out for himself. He was quick and strong, and felt he didn't have to take anything from the "Heinies" or the "Polacks." Sometimes his father joked about a bruise John couldn't conceal. "Ah, baseball is a rough game," he would say with a laugh. John kept his own counsel in that regard; he was afraid his father might not approve, but he was never sure. Dad could wink an eye at some things.

Now, every Sunday morning, John went to church. At the door he left his father and went to sit with his own grade. Sister sat in their midst, with an eagle eye for any radical departure from the normal squirming mass of young bodies. They watched the rise and flow of the Mass with bobbing attention, dropped their pennies, rattled their rosaries, wriggled through the unknown land of the sermon. They were all still for a moment when the organ broke into the introductory phrases of a hymn, and then launched themselves upon it with more gusto than precision.

First Communion time brought responsibilities. The Catechism lessons seemed endless. The chief hurdle was the long list of commandments, "First I am the Lord thy God," down to "Thou shalt not covet thy neighbor's goods." Sometimes, on the playground, more knowing boys discussed "Thou shalt not commit adultery" and "Thou shalt not covet thy neighbor's wife." John listened at the edge of the knot of sniggering faces. The talk disturbed him.

He brought the problem to his father. "Go long with you," his father said. "You're too young yet to trouble about these things. We'll talk about them later. Love God now, and keep your heart in peace. And say your prayers."

At last the children were almost letter perfect in their Catechism, with a little prompting here and there. Young as they were, they all knew what it meant to receive the Lord. He was "their heavenly food, the pledge of eternal life."

John made his first confession in the warm darkness of the box. The green curtain billowed behind him. He had a clear conception of right and wrong. He could recall moments when without permission he had filched a handful of raisins or cookies, and other times when he had let a curse word slip out among his intimates. There was more of demonstrative masculinity in him than there was of malice, but John was sure he had willed the offence.

On the morning of the great day, scrubbed and shining within and without, John sat among the other boys in the front pews. Each boy had a pink rose pinned on the white lapel of his jacket. Across the aisle, the girls of the class wore angelic faces under the mist of their veils. Freckled and ordinary faces, in the drab light of the classroom or street, were raised to beauty for a morning. Small as they were, the children had come to church fasting for the first time. This, too, marked the morning with a significance which in itself lent a further touch of exaltation. They all felt stiff and solemn—for once they did not resemble a can of fishing worms.

The tinkle of the bell announced the moment of Communion. They bowed their heads and chorused. "O Lord, I am not worthy that Thou shouldst enter under my roof, say but the word and my soul shall be healed."

Softly the organ took up the same pattern. "O Lord, I am not worthy." There was a hush in the church. The neat, white-clad lines of childish figures approached the marble railing. John's father and mother, like most of the other parents, watched their child with a hint of tears in their eyes. They remembered the little church in Kilglass and their own First Communion, the green-black trees heavy with morning mist, the sky with the promise of Easter about it. It seemed only yesterday, that morning on which they had sealed their compact with the Lord.

The church on John's First Communion day was throbbing with memories: the plains of Poland, the picturesque atmosphere of Trier and Cologne. In a few moments Mass was over; the congregation were on their feet: children and grownups. The organ soared:

> Holy God, we praise Thy name.
> Lord of all, we bow before Thee.

The window frames rattled with the sound.

The day was like a dream to John. Breakfast at home was a rite this morning. A table had been laid in the living room in the light of the bow window. The cloth was of heavy Irish linen embroidered with a pattern of roses and shamrocks. There was a vase of jonquils on it, and all the best china and cut glass. John's two sisters—the pallid Mary, and Anna with her tangle of gold curls—looked at John with wide, serious eyes. His mother and father were radiant.

The neighbors came to snap John's picture in the back garden, and then he went back to the church to have a second picture taken with the other boys and girls of the class. The solemnity of the day unbent a little. Father McKeever jested with them. The little girls were in a passion of titters; the boys blushed and picked at the grass, laughed and nudged one another.

All the old bromides were used in taking the picture: "Look at the birdie! Don't be afraid you'll crack your face if you smile." The shutter clicked at last and the scene was recorded for posterity. John never forgot the day, the first link in a golden chain that bound him to the altar.

It was hard to step down from the exaltation of first communion into ordinary life again. The warm school days were drawing to a close. Summer called. John looked out the window in a dream more often than he looked in his books.

The end of school came at last, but it brought a burden of pain and worry to John and his family. One evening he and the boys along the street were playing hunting in Africa. The realities of May in Newark were all about them. The light was harsh, the air had a taint of smoke and burning refuse. "That was from 'Joisey' City," everyone said, "not from Newark."

But to John the streets did not exist. He was in Africa moving through the thick, harsh grass. He was going down toward the water hole; tigers were lapping through its scum of green slime.

Little Harvey Phillips, the only colored boy in the gang, was John's gunbearer. He could see the dusky hue of Harvey's face, and his rolling eyes sent a shiver of more intense reality along John's spine. That thicket of thorn—they must get through it for the best shot. The two hunters slipped through the hedge. Harvey was trailing his BB gun, no longer an air gun but the elephant gun on which the life of the whole village depended. They were almost at the water hole now. Harvey was creeping through the last small twigs of the hedge, pulling the gun after him. John turned, he heard a pop, an incredible pain lanced through his right eye. The trigger of the gun had caught in a twig. John was writhing on the grass pressing his hand over his eye. He could hear Harvey sobbing.

"John, John, I didn't mean to shoot! John . . ." The little colored boy was weak with terror. He threw the gun from him, climbed the nearest fence, and ran toward home. He would be blamed, he knew it.

John's father lifted the screaming boy and ran with him to the couch in the front room. The doctor came, and the red-faced policeman from the block pushed his way through the angry crowd at the front steps. "Now then. What's it all about."

Through his pain and tears John's voice was weak and persistent. "It wasn't Harvey's fault, I tell you. We were playing hunting in Africa, the BB gun must have caught on a twig. It wasn't Harvey's fault."

It was weeks before the eye healed. John was himself again, and the neighborhood feeling against Harvey had evaporated. But through the whole long summer John's eye pained him. Sometimes a mist would form before it. Then the doctor fitted him with glasses. Now he could be called "old four-eye." He would have to remember to take off his glasses when he was dared to knock the chip off someone's shoulder. Destiny was already playing a part in his life. The weakness of his right eye would one day keep him from a Navy chaplaincy and a different pattern of life in the Pacific.

At home, now, Dad and Mother talked about the war. The Kaiser was a bully; he had smashed his way through the towns of Belgium. They talked of Cardinal Mercier who had opposed the Kaiser's military power with a determined spirit. Priests and nuns had been sent to prison. The great Cathedral at Louvain was shattered by German guns.

In 1916 the shadow of the green island also intruded itself upon their feelings. John heard his father and mother using strange names: Padraic Pearse, Plunkett. The Irish had risen in Dublin against their English masters. "England's difficulty was Ireland's opportunity." The Easter Martyrs, John's father called the men who had been shot for their part in the abortive rebellion.

John warmed to his father's indignation. The English, too, were bullies like the Kaiser. That conviction had no time to become set. The *Lusitania* was sunk and a wave of indignation carried the United States into the war. The streets of Newark were gay with bunting and flags. Everyone was excited. Along Twelfth Street Irish and German and Polish boys were called up in the draft.

John had flashing memories of parades. Sitting in the car with his father and mother, he watched the khaki lines marching off to France. The bands were playing a fresh tune full of dash and spirit, "Over there, over there."

Now John and his friends invented a new game. The green slopes of the park were the fields of France. Feats of incredible derringdo pushed them on the road to Berlin. Kaiser Bill was on the run. . . .

Yet the old pieties kept pace and importance with new excitements. One of the most memorable days of the year was the feast of Saint Patrick. For a month before March 17th the nuns drilled even the smallest children in Irish songs and dances. John's father made a special trip to New York for Irish bacon. A pot of real Shamrock and green moss arrived from Roscommon. Mama was baking fresh buns, and a huge cake peppered with green candies.

The records of John McCormack were dusted off: "Believe Me If All Those Endearing Young Charms," "My Snowy Breasted Pearl." A vague longing for the past and perfection. They grew sad and sentimental with "When Irish Eyes Are Smiling" and "Where the River Shannon Flows."

Saint Patrick's morning they all went off to Mass. John had a silk shamrock stuck in his lapel, a green-gilt paper harp pasted on it. It must be Tara's harp, John thought.

Father McKeever preached an orotund sermon on Saint Patrick. John's heart responded as he heard the throbbing strophes of the hymn:

> All hail to Saint Patrick,
> Who brought to our mountains
> The gift of God's grace,
> The sweet light of His love.
> All praise to the shepherd
> Who showed us the fountains
> That rise in the heart
> Of the Saviour above.

Father McKeever wore the best white vestments, used on Christmas and Easter. Why didn't he wear green, John wondered. He asked Dad about it. "Patrick was a confessor, a great confessor," John's father told him. "And the liturgy says the priest will wear white for a confessor." He shook his head with a chuckle. "But I well remember Canon Connell in me father's time. He flouted all the directions and always came out of the sacristy with his best green bib and tucker." John couldn't understand these difficult things, but he was pleased to see his father laughing so heartily at his recollection, even wiping his eyes with the back of his hand.

When the Mass was over, all the Irish gathered on the steps of the church. There conversation recalled memories of the "Green Island." They were descendants of Irish kings, were they not? They boasted of their ancestors and their childhood. Those not of Irish origin couldn't understand them. To those outside the pale, the Irish seemed to have an emotional split. They lived in America, loved it, and gave their sons to its quarrels; but their fondest memories were of Ireland, of Cork and Killarney, Cashel and Dublin, and the wild bays of Galway.

Ireland was the pastoral dream in the heart of every man. It was the land of quietness, the land of spices, of herds, of dark streams and green, green meadows stained with purple heather and yellow gorse. There a man might wander on the lazy hills disturbed by no noise but the wind and the boom of the heavy-bagged bees. Cabin fires breathed out the smell of moss. At nighttime there the storytellers gathered. In the leaping flames old dreams materialized: the giants battled in the cattle raid on Cooley, Maeve and her maidens queened it, and out from the roots of the white thorn came trooping the little people. On week ends at the crossroads there was dancing, fierce and full of fire, and soft voices saying a lingering good night at the silvered cottages when the dance was over.

These things the country boys and girls never forgot. In Australia, Canada, or America the dreams emerged on each Saint Patrick's day. In their children the dream would be a sentimental nostalgia, and in their children's children a half-humorous memory. The dreams of the new land would efface the soft idyll for those who had never moved through its lyrical air.

John caught the essence of the dream from his father. It seemed to be more valid than the reality he saw around him. A sentimental cast in his spirit made him fertile ground for planting. It was something to be Irish; something finer still to be both Irish and American. Ireland was the dream, America the reality; Ireland was the place to visit, to grow soft about; America was the place to live. They were all proud of their divided unity—the Fighting 69th was often their talk in the war years. Those of Irish descent took pride in Father Duffy and Irishmen who kept alive the old heroism in the new land.

These ideas were felt more than they were rationalized in John's young mind. They gave him a peculiar spark and a kind of belligerence. He cultivated quick humor and a swift resentment. His dry comments enlarged his influence on the playground; glasses or no glasses, he kept the chip precariously balanced on his shoulder. In his dreams he saw himself a wit like Mr. Dooley or a fighter like Jack Sullivan; in his softer moments he pictured himself a hero of the stamp of Father Duffy. On a white horse he rode down the lines comforting the men, encouraging them to heroic deeds.

The priest-hero was an old story to John. From the hills of Roscommon his father had brought glowing recollections of hunted men of God who had lived in the hills and the hedges and comforted their people. John's dreams came to a realistic focus in the sixth grade. There his imaginative world merged imperceptibly with the real world about him.

Events and people played a part in the change. Sister Anna Clarita was his new teacher. She had a casual way about her, which revealed and brought to focus the wise realities behind maxims that had seemed old saws or pious platitudes. John noticed this first of all in the way she said her prayers. They neither scampered nor lagged. The tone of her voice was conversational. She thought the words while her tongue formed them. Too she had an understanding way with children and never stepped down to their level with the kind of condescension which makes a child conscious of an invasion from an alien world. She was also sympathetic, and her sympathy had a strong twist of humor in it. It was a strengthening sympathy which John knew well at first hand.

John's class had been studying geography; the lesson for the day was on the British Isles. To John the capital of these was not London, but Dublin. Boundaries, rivers, lakes—he had them at his tongue's end. Waterford, Tipperary, Clare, Limerick, Cork, and Kerry. Some of the names were like poems, old poems his father had taught him. John could see the other children watching him, amazed and envious. The mention of Lough Derg emboldened him. He put up his hand. "Yes, John?" Sister Anna Clarita queried.

John stood up at the side of his low desk "It's a beautiful lake," he announced. "My father said so. He and my mother courted each other about its shores."

The antique word intrigued the children. Looking down at them, John saw them bent over their desktops with laughter. John's face puffed with fury. He flung himself into his seat.

"Now, now," Sister observed in a soft voice. "I'm afraid you all laughed at the wrong place." Her voice was factual. "Over here when we speak of young people in love we say they are 'keeping company,' but in Ireland they wouldn't use those words. They use the word 'courting,' just as Shakespeare did and the great poets of the sixteenth and seventeenth centuries. And in fact it's the more beautiful word."

John felt his rage ebbing from him. The experience, however, taught him caution.

It was in the sixth grade, too, that John had his first extended encounter with the world of music. Many of the children on Twelfth Street studied some music with Marion Wirth. She herself was almost young enough to be one of them. When John's mother first suggested music lessons to her son he was not enthusiastic. "Aw, that's for sisses." His mother saw the determination in the eyes behind John's glasses and the hard set of the boy's jaw.

"Oh, I shouldn't say that. Paderewski's not a sissy, but a fine strapping man. And he is the Premier of Poland. And," his mother continued, "Tom Moore was a man's man, but everyone loved to hear him play his songs and sing them. But wait awhile, dear, you needn't take the lessons if you don't want them."

"I'd rather play baseball." One hand touched his glasses with an unconscious gesture.

Mrs. Washington said no more. Nor was it necessary, John was turning her words over in his mind. The glasses he wore had filled him with a special need to be thought a regular guy. There was a hint of swagger in his masculinity and this, under any sudden stress, became positive belligerence. Without his glasses John did not see well, but he forced himself into positions of honor or danger without mercy to himself.

In baseball, for example, he was not meant to be a pitcher.

That called for special talent, and he just didn't have it. Very well, he would make himself a catcher. The mask would cover up his glasses and protect them. They would also be hidden. The catcher's mask came to be a symbol for him. It was the mask of normality and it was also like the invisible helmet Siegfried wore. It made him indistinguishable from his teammates while he labored through the game. With constant practice at the cost of swollen fingers John managed to hold his place.

Yet, he confessed to himself, music did attract him. In the early spring evenings on his way home from school he heard the soft echo of Marion's piano following him down the street. No lesson; she was playing for her own amusement. There were no lights on in the house, yet her fingers evoked melody after melody. It would be something to be able to do that. . . .

John's mother was happy to hear his announcement, "I've decided I will take lessons from Marion, Ma."

The lessons were harder than games, John found. It was a delight to be able to play his first melody, but practice was boring. He had to sit still, and his imagination of what he should be able to do leaped ahead of his accomplishments. He saw himself playing like Paderewski.

John's sixth year at school also brought his elevation to the stature of an altar boy. Sister taught him the difficult Latin prayers. John learned them parrot fashion. *Et introibo ad altare Dei*, with which the priest opened the Mass, was a beautiful sentence. It meant, "I shall go up to the altar of God." The server's response was of equal beauty, "To God who gives joy to my youth." But there was no translation of either sentence on the server's card, and John learned his responses without full awareness of their meaning. The boys thought it good form to race through each response with the speed of light. They said, *Ad Deumquilaetificat* in one breath and one word, and *Juventutemmeum* in another. The Confiteor was a millrace of sound. Each vied with his fellow server in rushing to the end of it. They contested, too, for the honor of being the server who would ring the bell. While Father McKeever vested in the commodious priest's sacristy, there was often in the other sacristy across the sanctuary considerable jostling and debate among the servers for the place of honor. The handling of the wine, the ringing of the bells with a great jangle, these were honorable things to an altar boy, worth fighting for. Behind the angelic façade which the congregation saw there were rivalries, envies, more than casual levity.

The very restraint and solemnity of the boys' position lent an air of the ridiculous to the smallest things. If the bell ringer nudged his bells into sound before the precise moment set, both little servers were like leaves in a high wind of silent laughter. Any unusual noise in the church, a mistake, a grimace, the slightest thing made them quiver.

The pious ladies of the Altar and Rosary Society might be deceived by the angelic faces of the boys emerging from the sacristy, but the old sacristan was more to the point when she said, "Ah yes, they look like angels to be sure *sometimes,* but there's a good bit of the divvil in them most of the time."

John appeared to be much like the rest of them. It was the essence of his own psychology not to be thought different. Yet at Benediction, sometimes, he felt a certain sweetness in the music, and his heart was enlarged with a sentiment deeper than laughter or pain. He pondered this in his prayers. After communion, in particular, he often felt something that was almost like the touch of a hand. Then, the words of the Our Father and the Hail Mary took on a fuller meaning and intensity.

Gradually he came to feel that God was calling him to the priesthood. At home he could admit the impulse without concealment. His mother and father were happy that it should be so.

After some thought, John confided his secret to Sister Anna Clarita. "I'm going to be a priest, Sister." His voice hesitated. "But I'd rather no one knew about it but you and me."

"Very well," Sister replied. "It will be our secret. But you must be good, John, specially good, if you mean to be a priest. I'll pray for you, too, every morning when I make my meditation." Her rosary clinked in her fingers. "And now remember it will take lots of study. A priest must be a man of books and a man of God."

"I'll betcha I know my Catechism best of all the confirmation class."

Sister laughed. It made John feel good to hear the sound. Her eyes twinkled.

"That's fine, John. I'll depend on you. So many of the boys and girls turn into lumps when the bishop asks them a question."

John lived up to his promise. His father and mother helped him. He was not satisfied merely to know the answers, he could explain them, too, in simpler words.

Sister was proud of him on confirmation night. When the bishop asked, "How many venial sins make a mortal sin?" John was quick to point out that the question was impossible to answer. "Venial sins are slight sins," he said. "They cannot add up to a mortal sin by which we lose the grace of God." John saw Sister Anna Clarita and the bishop smiling. Their silent commendation added even more pleasure to the occasion.

The bishop's talk was a homely exposition of the meaning of confirmation. It was the sacrament of spiritual manhood, and spiritual power. In a special way, the Holy Spirit came with his gifts of wisdom, understanding, counsel, fortitude, knowledge, piety, and the fear of the Lord—those gifts which were necessary for manhood and womanhood amid the trials of the world.

John walked up to the bishop's faldstool, his heart throbbing with excitement. Before him was the full majesty of the Roman Church. The gold miter and the glittering crosier clothed that majesty with hieratic and almost Byzantine splendor. John felt the hard steps under his knees. The bishop's fingers were on his forehead tracing a cross there, smooth with oil.

"Patritius, I sign thee with the sign of the cross, and I confirm thee with the chrism of salvation." The bishop gave John's cheek a light tap. That had special meaning to the boy. It symbolized the suffering he must be ready to endure for his faith. It would have seemed merely symbolic a few years past. The Church had come a long way from the ages of the martyrs, such as young Agnes and Sebastian. But now in the *Catholic News* John read of new martyrs in Mexico. Who knew what the future would bring? On this confirmation night the boy felt strong and willing to endure any hazard of the future.

John's year in Grade Seven helped to decide many things for him. It was accepted that he would go toward the priesthood. To this end he would enter Seton Hall in Orange, New Jersey, and take his high school and college courses there. Then he would go on to the major seminary at Darlington for his theological course.

The years in high school and the three years of his college course beyond that would permit John every freedom the boys of his age had. It would be up to him to persevere in his calling through all the blandishments of the world and the surges of his own desires. Final decisions were far away, locked in some solemn moments of an unknown future. For the present it was enough to enjoy existence.

It snowed a lot that year. Coming home from school the boys pelted one another with snowballs. John was happy to have Anna by his side in the frays. She was his shadow now, holding his books or rolling pellets for him to throw. He was the sort of brother any girl would take pride in. He was a leader among the boys at school, a top student, and one of the chief altar boys —things splendid in themselves and worthy of admiration. But it was John's kindness which lent a luster to his accomplishments. He was good to Anna, companionable, witty, courteous, all heart.

John's virtues were brought home to Anna that winter with particular force. One evening when he came into the house he said, "Ma, I'm sick." She felt his forehead. It was hot. "You must have a cold."

"I have, and my throat is *so* sore."

"Into bed with you, then! Don't forget to gargle with Listerine. I'll rub your throat and chest with Mentholatum and give you a glass of hot lemonade. You'll be all right in the morning."

But in the morning John's cheeks were crimson with fever. He refused to eat anything, and now and then he gave a slight groan as he tossed about in the big bed.

Anna heard her mother calling the doctor on the telephone. She was putting on her coat and hat for the short walk to school. It had snowed again in the night; the plows were out, and flying shovels made a sharp scraping noise in the street.

All morning Anna was inattentive at her lessons. She could think of nothing but John. How was he now? She ran home at noon for lunch. What she saw in her mother's face frightened her. Mrs. Washington had been crying. Anna knew John was worse.

In the evening the doctor called again. He came into the living room after a careful examination of his patient, his expression grave, and he shook his head. "I can't seem to get the boy's fever down. It's a quinsy he has, and if we can't drop that fever, his case will be serious by morning. Continue to use ice packs. And give him two of these pills every hour. Call me if there is any change." Anna caught the frightened glance passing between her father and mother.

By nine o'clock John was unconscious. Anna watched her father putting on his coat in the living room. His shoulders were slack with discouragement, and he left the house wiping his eyes on the back of his hand.

The doctor came before her father had returned with Father McKeever. They all stood in John's room. Mrs. Washington was preparing a small table there. She spread a fresh linen cloth and carefully placed on it two candles, a crucifix, and a little glass dish with balls of fresh cotton. Father McKeever breathed kindness and encouragement. Under the heavy wings of his eyebrows his face was serene.

Father McKeever put on his purple stole and opened his worn black Ritual. "Peace be unto this house and all who dwell therein." Then he raised his right hand, holding the sprinkler-top bottle of holy water, and blessed the sick boy and the four walls of the room: "Sprinkle me, O Lord, with hyssop and I shall be made clean; Wash me and I shall be made whiter than snow."

The ancient Latin prayers which followed the psalm were a voice of comfort in the room.

Then Father McKeever anointed the senses of the dying boy: the eyes, the ears, the nostrils, the lips, hands, and feet.

With a sense of apostolic optimism and hope one of the prayers struck the ears of the sorrowing family.

"Let us pray! Lord God, Who hast spoken by Thine Apostle James, saying: Is any man sick among you? Let him call in the priests of the Church and let them pray over him, anointing him with oil in the name of the Lord; and the prayer of faith shall save the sick man, and the Lord will raise him up and if he be in sins, they shall be forgiven him: cure, we beseech Thee, O Our Redeemer, by the grace of the Holy Ghost, the ailments of this sick man; heal his wounds and forgive his sins; drive out from him all pains of body and mind and mercifully restore to him full health, both inwardly and outwardly; that having recovered by the help of Thy mercy, he may once more have strength to take up his former duties. Who with the Father and the same Holy Ghost, livest and reignest God, world without end. Amen."

The face of the boy on the pillow looked flushed and swollen. The soft response of the prayers which followed the anointing filled the little room with the resplendent power of the communion of saints.

Before leaving, Father McKeever spoke to John's father and mother in the parlor. "Don't give up now. Remember this sacrament of anointing is also a sacrament of physical healing. I have blessed John with the relic of the Little Flower. Be brave."

"God's will be done," Frank Washington said. "John is such a good boy, such a good boy." He put his arm around his wife.

"He's none too good for God," Mary Washintgon cried.

In the morning Anna found her father and mother smiling.

"He's much better," her mother was exulting. "Thanks be to God! The fever is going down."

Later, when he was well, John himself spoke of his illness to Anna. "I guess I nearly put on my wings," he observed with a quick laugh. "But God must have kept me here for something. I'll try to discover what it is."

Anna detected a new seriousness in John from this point forward. He still wore his carefree outer mask. His jokes were more frequent than ever, he was still devoted to being a regular guy, but Anna could see that his prayers were longer, his kindness to all the family was intensified.

Francis, Leo, and Tom sometimes quarreled. If their father was not at home, young John took them in hand. "There'll be no fights in this house," he warned them. "If you must fight, come out in the back yard and put on the gloves with me. I'll take some of the fight out of you." The boys usually grinned at his words, and made up or dropped their differences. John was looking down at them with a twinkle in his eye, but they knew he meant what he said.

His mother, too, saw a change in her son. He came in earlier from play quite often now. "I'll help you, Mom," he volunteered. He would rattle the plates in the cupboard, lay the table, and pop in and out of the living room with wisecracks and teasing stories which brought a hint of color to the anemic face of Mary.

On Saturday John would take young Edmund with him on hikes and to the baseball field. "You've lots of shopping to do, Ma. Edmund will get under your feet. I'll take him along with me." Mrs. Washington, with a smile, watched the two figures going down the street. Her first born and her baby! John had moderated his quick walk to suit his little brother's steps. John has a tender heart, she thought. Edmund seems happier with him than anyone else.

John's last year at St. Rose's ran by too swiftly. Almost before he knew it he was catching the bus to Seton Hall. He had a paper route now. With that and his new interests at the Hall, Twelfth Street saw less of him.

He would dash into the house for supper, throw his books and catcher's mitt into the corner, and rush into the kitchen with a quick hug for his mother. The lively house became more fully alive with his coming.

Sometimes he brought his new pal, Jimmie O'Connell, with him. Then supper would send all the children into flurries of laughter. On Friday nights the two boys went out for a walk. No more study until Sunday night. The Latin books and themes lay neglected in the corner. Usually the two boys managed to turn themselves in the direction of the pool halls around Orange and Roosevelt Avenues, where the balls made patterns and music on the green tables. Cigarettes came out of hiding and dangled from the corners of young lips.

Pool halls had a bad name among reformers, too often content to condemn without suggesting other amusements. The halls were often pictured as haunts of sin and vice, but they were actually far more innocent than reformers hoped. They kept the boys off the street; they were the clubs of those groups who had not a great deal of money to spend on their pleasures. Among these, John was noted for his sharp play and in the parlance of the time was said to "shake a mean cue."

To Jimmie O'Connell his friend John Washington was the peak of regularity. John loved games, weenie roasts, pool, and long walks. He went to Communion every week, but except for his contempt of shady stories and shady language, there was no sign about him, not the slightest outward hint, which indicated he had set his mind and heart on being a priest.

Jimmie and John also became mad dancers, another sign that they were regular guys. Public dance halls were plentiful in Newark. Some of them were run with responsibility, but many were not. One exception was the Irish-American Dance Hall on Central and Broad streets. On Saturday and Sunday nights this hall became intensely alive. To it thronged the professional Irishmen and Irishmen of every sort, comparing their false nostalgias with true Irish spontaneity and striving for conversational supremacy in little knots at the edge of the floor. Some of the onlookers were ward politicians who used the occasion to build up their fences, but most of them were young boys and girls of good families who loved to gather with their own kind and race. Sometimes they came with their fathers and mothers. Most of the boys went stag, though occasionally they brought a girl from their own neighborhood. Everyone found a few hours of amusing chatter and Celtic glamor, endless reels and waltzes.

In preparation for the invasion of this world the two boys saved their money and took dancing lessons in advance. For them there would be no stumbling about the floor to the laughter of the colleens.

At their first appearance Jimmie and John acted the part of old hands. They knew how to move in time with the music and had already mastered the intricacies of the one-step, the fox trot, the waltz, and the schottische. Under the green and white streamers of the ceiling they hopped about with all the best dancers. In the so-called moonlight waltzes, in which the lights were dimmed and the great turning ball in the center of the room sent out sparkles of refracted light, they floated like thistledown.

In their approach to learning the two boys pursued opposite paths. John was a traditionalist in the best sense of the term. He accepted authorities in any field, without question. His reasoning was deductive. Jimmie was experimental in his methods. Traditions and authorities he accepted if and when facts proved them to be correct. The minds of the two boys made a fine contrast; their tastes and amusements a perfect agreement.

Long walks in the early hours of the fall evenings were frequent. Jimmie would drop over from his house on Eleventh Street, and he and John would call Tom Meehan to join them. Often they walked to Eagle Rock and back, singing, making jokes, and arguing about everything under the sun.

To the three boys, strolling along under the lengthening shadows of the trees, life was intense because they were participating in it with both mind and body. The rhythm of their swift pace made their blood sing; their minds were stimulated by talk of sports and studies and their varying outlook on mice and men.

John's sister Mary had never been well. In winter she huddled over the gas grate; in summer her face gleamed pallidly in the darkness of the curtained parlor. In her own way she had been a boon to the Washingtons; she evoked whatever tenderness lay dormant within them. They were more conscious of Mary than they were of any other member of the family.

Her death at fifteen, during John's last year in high school, was not unexpected. They had all intensified hope, and they had prayed hard that she might be spared them. Standing at Mary's grave, John's misted eyes marked his father's arms about his mother's shaking shoulders. He joined in the prayers with a kind of emptiness. But he felt partly consoled in the knowledge that now he would have Mary to pray for him in the difficult years ahead. She had suffered with the withdrawn humility of a saint, and the boy could not doubt that she had walked into the reward of light and peace—"perpetual light," in which they could all hope to join her one day.

Yet in spite of these supernatural intuitions the experience was a distinct shock to John. Healthy as he was, death seemed standing at his very shoulder in this first invasion of the family circle. Looking at the dear faces gathered under the light at home, after the funeral, the boy wondered which of them would next depart.

This contact with death led John to plunge into wider activities and deeper study. Seton Hall was a small school at the time. Everyone knew everyone else. The classes themselves were small enough to compel a man to stand comparison with the best of his fellows.

John found it no real strain to stay on the level of the last group. He had a talent for languages which might easily have grown into splendid scholarship. The boy knew and admitted to himself that he had intellectual powers but not intellectual taste. Outside his classes he had no wish to be pointed out as a highbrow. In his passion for conformity, he preferred to be known among his fellows as an ace pool player or a good catcher. He had much more desire to use his wit for the amusement of others than for himself.

This attitude revealed itself in many overt ways. John had shown a marked ability in school plays, a talent which might easily have marked him with the brand of the aesthete. He avoided that possibility by developing comedy roles. In these he was a success on the stage and off. His playing of the part of Bulldog Drummond's foppish companion in one play was considered by his fellows a perfect satire on the finical.

He was so adroit at comedy parts that everyone was surprised when he accepted the role of the Lord High Justice in a serious play, *The Illustrious Life and Death of Thomas More*. Was the gang about to lose its best pool player? Perhaps John was changing.

On the night of the play they all found themselves mistaken in their surmises. John played his role to the hilt. He was so serious, in fact, that he put the martyr in the shade with an almost dead-pan dryness. At first the dramatic coach could not understand why John's every move brought cackles of laughter from the audience of students and parents, but before the final curtain the hawk-eyed director discovered the reason. Strapped about John's left wrist, which dangled from his gorgeous Tudor robe, was a shining wrist watch. And John was munching a cud of gum. These things more than enhanced John's prestige among his fellows. They showed their esteem in the way boys will, by constant ribbing, most of which John took and returned in a good-natured way. A thick hide was one of the prime qualities cultivated by his gang.

He was, however, unduly sensitive about his name. "Washington!" a boy would say insinuatingly. "That's a colored name, isn't it?"

John went on the defensive at once. "It's Irish," he would explain. "My father and mother are both Irish."

"Are you sure?"

"Yes, I'm sure, and if you don't believe me, I'll knock your block off."

Most boys, observing the storm signals, would quit at this point. Bolder spirits pressed their advantage, and sometimes in the showers after baseball practice they pretended to detect a dark streak running along John's spine.

On one occasion the matter came up in class, to John's extreme chagrin. Professor Scavone, in history class, was taking down the names of his new pupils at the outset of the school year. When John answered, "John P. Washington," the professor paused and looked at the boy.

"This is no time for jokes!"

John was almost purple with embarrassment. "But I'm not joking," he said. "My name is John P. Washington and the P. stands for Patrick."

"Very well, then," the professor replied. "I'm sorry I questioned you, but I have never known an Irishman with that name before, though I can plainly see you are of Hibernian vintage."

John heard his friends laughing. It did not help to make him fond of history.

The serious qualities at the bottom of John's character remained very much in evidence, but he concealed them from everyone except his family and the nuns. In consequence, all his close friends at the Hall grew hilarious to hear that John was destined for the seminary. He first broke the news to Jimmie O'Connell and Tom Meehan. They responded to his announcement with unbelieving faces.

"Are you kidding?" Jimmie asked.

"No, I'm not." John was dead serious, Jimmie saw. He must mean it.

"O.K. then. You may feel like this now, but you'll never make the grade."

"What'll you bet?"

"How about a silk hat?"

John was laughing now. "A silk hat! It's a deal." The two boys shook hands to seal the bargain.

"I'll not only win that hat," John boasted, "but I'll wear it when you marry some redhead. Maybe that will learn you!"

Jimmie might have expected John's announcement to make an immediate difference. He was surprised that it didn't.

In what time remained to John at the Hall he pursued his wisecracking way.

In July, with the gang, he went to Belmar for a week. He attended all the local dances and was loudest and roughest in the casual horseplay on the beach.

September, 1931, found John settled in at Darlington. The seminary, the boy discovered, was one of the most unusual places of its kind in the world. There were fourteen hundred acres of land surrounding it. Toward the east the ground fell away toward a nine-hole golf course. Beyond that, the land sloped up again to the Ramapo hills, which formed the approximate boundary of the estate—fourteen hundred acres dotted with irregular patches of woods, a wild tangle of beeches, oaks, and maples. The place was only an hour's ride from Newark, but it seemed miles from anything. This sense of strangeness and distance was magnified by the people of the district, known as the "Jackson Whites," who displayed *Tobacco Road* qualities unmatched outside the Ozarks, or the remote regions of the Deep South.

The seminary buildings were extraordinary. Stanford White had designed the central hall. Originally it had been built by a California tycoon, and was a near replica of Darlington Castle.

Had John lived in this house his first year, he might have been overwhelmed with its grandeur. It was quite a change from the modest atmosphere he knew on Twelfth Street, or the brownstone dowdiness of Seton Hall. John actually found himself housed in the caretaker's home, more modest in design. It had been built by the farmer who originally owned the land, and probably reflected his conception of grandeur, since it was a cross between Georgian and American Civil-War Planter styles.

John learned to make his own bed and shine his own shoes. He also bore his proper share of the dusting and polishing of the dorm. In addition to these things, he learned to wait on table in the big dining room at the main hall. What seemed strangest to him, now, was that he was required to wear his cassock day in and day out. It was a while before he got used to that flapping noise about his ankles.

The junior hall, or the "rookery," as it was known among the boys, was several blocks down from the hall. The rising bell jangled at five-thirty in the morning. Then there was a rush to the bathrooms, a quick shower and shave, after which they all trooped up to the "castle" for meditation and Mass. Monsignor McLoughlin, affectionately known as "Schlitz," was always waiting, watch in hand, at the door of the great hall, which had been turned into a temporary chapel.

The moment the last boy had filed into his stall, morning prayers began. The rounded phrases of the Latin poured out, thanking God for the new day, begging His grace in it.

At the conclusion of the prayers, the reader for the week read out his first point of meditation, a moral and theological lesson on the saint, or the feast, of the day. Silence fell in the big room; young men turned the first point over in their minds, thinking of its lessons, applying them in a practical way to their own lives and the future. In thoughts of the saints, or Our Lady, they caught varied views of the face of Christ. To form their minds and lives on Him, to be the other Christs, was the sum of their dedication.

In the silence the flame of the sanctuary lamp danced like David before the Ark of the Covenant. Outside, the light climbed into the sky, flooding the windows with shafts of crimson. The pipes of the organ, the carvings on roof and pillars throbbed with life and color. Birds sang in the woods beyond.

When the half-hour of meditation was ended, the Mass began. Here, among future priests, it had an added solemnity and intimacy. They all knew Latin and followed the mellow text of the Missal—prayers not unworthy of the great mystery they were celebrating.

After Mass there was Thanksgiving, which lasted for fifteen minutes. This time was the longest period of the day. As healthy young men should be, they were all hungry. The moment the handbell tinkled they hurried to the dining room, a short distance down the hall. On ordinary mornings there was spiritual reading during breakfast. Dodging the glances of the professors at the high table, the boys made jokes in stolen whispers.

After a brief Thansckgiving in the chapel they all rushed out to the pergola for a quick smoke and the morning's repartee. Black-cloaked figures fell into little knots of friends who compared notes on the details of the past evening. Those who smoked puffed furiously on their cigarettes. The interval was short, for they must hurry back to their rooms, sweep them, make their beds, polish the floors, and then rush up the hill again for the first class at nine.

Their schedule was heavy, John discovered without undue dismay. Moral and Dogmatic Theology, Canon Law, Liturgy, Church History, Plain Chant, Pastoral Theology. The texts were in Latin, and some of the lectures as well. Casual Latin in high school and college had not prepared John for the use of that language as a ready tool. He had to force his attention in every class, and his mind now was at full stretch in following lectures in a strange language which bristled with philosophical facts and endless authorities.

There were two ends in view, John saw with great clarity. One was the following of Christ, by means of which self-perfection and the selfless service of men came into being. The other was the acquisition of learning and strength of will, which ministered to the first end. Christ and the Church were one. Knowledge of Our Lord's historical life was a *sine qua non,* but the extension of His personality through time was the Church. This, too, demanded a ready knowledge of the Church's growth in doctrine, and a study of her history and holiness.

The courses and disciplines of the seminary life were a training and protection for the years of service to the Master. Love and balance were necessary. One without the other eventuated in a half priest. Balance alone produced worldly prudence. Love without balance had a tendency to become eccentricity or instability. The key to both was humility. Not the sour humility of a bent head—that was a purely outward show. Real humility had no falseness about it, required no particular manner. Rather, it consisted in knowing human littleness in comparison with God. Everything John Washington had come to be was the free gift of God. His life, his talent, his calling, his daily graces—these were all given. In himself, he thought of himself as nothing.

This idea suited well his passion for being a regular guy. The Church in her discipline at the seminary hoped her priests would become saints, but she asked for no singularity in demonstration of that sanctity.

John studied to perfect his mind; he was anxious for moral self-perfection, but outwardly he made it a point to appear unchanged. In the free time every afternoon he was one of the first on the baseball diamond. Between classes he gravitated toward a group of lively young men like himself.

McCue, Rush, Carey, Cunningham, Whalen, Martin, Byrne, and Curtin—the "Irish Saints," John called them. They gathered in the sunny pergola, hands in the pockets of their cassocks. They joked about the classes. Their talk was largely salted with sports news; when they indulged in philosophical wrangles their language was pungent. John was teased without mercy because his clincher in any argument, theological or otherwise, was that old phrase, "My father said so." At first the "sunny corner's gang" were almost afraid to tease him about this, but their faces showed their amusement at this quirk in their friend.

Behind the mask of daily routine John's spirit deepened. He learned to love his Lord with an intense personal love. There were many occasions when he wondered about himself. Was he doing all he could in self-dedication? He thought of the time he had nearly died. He thought of his dead sister. Did God call him to higher perfection? For a time he believed he ought to leave the seminary and join the Passionist Fathers.

John wrote to the superior of the Passionist Fathers in the East, setting forth his desire to join the community. In reply he received encouragement in his vocation, but he was told that for the moment the Passionist novitiate was full. John would have to wait.

This gave the boy time to reconsider the whole question. He took the matter to his spiritual advisor. The two men discussed it with thoroughness and common sense. Was John fitted to be a missionary? Had he the high qualities of mind and heart which would perfect his vocation? It was a thoughtful John who went away from the interview. It would be silly of him to pretend he was perfect in the life he was leading. Sometimes he chafed at the discipline, though not because he didn't see the reasons for it. He did—but he was young and bursting with life. Things of the moment carried him away into small infringements. How, then, could he hope to meet the more stringent demands of life in a missionary community? In the end the young man admitted that he had chosen wisely in remaining where he was.

On visiting days, John walked about the grounds with his father and mother. Seeing them infrequently, as he did, John realized how much he loved them both—their smiling faces, the hint of brogue, their rich humility and deep piety. They were a challenge to him. If he could achieve their goodness and endearing human qualities, his life in the priesthood would be rich in service.

Always Mary Washington brought gifts for John. To his delight they were usually food. "I baked a chicken for you and the boys, and an apple pie too. I knew you'd be hungry." This was a typical greeting to her son.

"You're the best cook in the world," John would tell her. "And how are the kids behaving since I'm not there to keep them in line?"

"Ah, they do very well," John's father reported with a sly smile. "Tom and Frank are lively, but they don't pick up black eyes like you used to do. That's perhaps because they don't play so much baseball."

All too soon the afternoon had melted away; all too soon the Buick was disappearing down the sweeping drive. In a few moments the bell would ring for Benediction. John carried his packages toward the hall. Of course he would share his loot with the "sunny corner's gang." And by the time they all added their packages together it would be a real feast.

John went unhurriedly along the path toward the hall. Around him the rich evening glow brought out every excellence in the landscape and buildings, and made the glass of the greenhouses into walls and roofs of fire.

In these moments John had flashes of genuine intuition. His discipline and the studies he pursued were good. It was all simple with the divine simplicity of life itself. At firsthand John was able to understand God the loving Father in the face of his own dear father. In the shining light of his mother's eyes he saw the maternal tenderness of Mary. That forbearance, too, like his mother's—a reluctance to judge any man or woman with harshness and her unfailing remark, "Only God knows."

Such moments of insight were balanced by small notes of failure. Among these was a strange block in John's nature, which made it impossible for him to learn to swim well. Part of it had to do with the glasses he wore. Without them he only half saw the world, or he saw it in a distorted way. Glasses were impossible in swimming. John refused to stick his neck out like a mud turtle in a fashion the wearing of glasses would have made imperative. Caught between his pride and his handicap, he watched the divers and swimmers with more than faint envy.

With the first warm afternoons of late May the young seminarians flocked to the "duckpond." Some of the more ambitious swimmers had built a simple cabana on the shores of the Ramapo, where they undressed and made ready for swimming. Slowly John put on his blue trunks and wandered down to the shore, leaving his glasses with his clothes. Coming out into the bright sunlight, he would blink a little. The water was still cold in this calm eddy of the river. Try as he would—and he tried with a fierce determination—the boy never felt at home in the alien element. If he tried to float, he went down like a stone; if he tried to swim, his knees or his feet scraped the bottom.

Day after day John stayed at his task. He began with the crawl; he couldn't learn it; he tried the side stroke, and the breast stroke; these, too, seemed to get him nowhere.

Dan Curtin helped John solve his problem. Without his glasses Dan was even more nearsighted than John; in fact, he was practically helpless. It was John himself who had affectionately called Dan the "blind man"—a name that had stuck to him among the "sunny corner's gang." In spite of his myopia Dan was strong and determined, and through sheer perseverance he had taught himself to swim well.

"It's not hard, John," Dan told his friend. "But you have to start out in an easy way. First get used to the water. After that the dog crawl is all you need. See!" He demonstrated the technique, splashing his powerful body in the water.

"If I had that hair mattress on my chest and shoulders I might be able to float," John replied. But he took Dan's advice and flopped and wallowed in the water with a great deal of puffing. In a few weeks he discovered that Dan's method really worked. Now he was able to propel himself for some distance close to the shore. He was afloat at last, without one noticeable scrape of the keel.

The climax of John's efforts came on the Feast of the Assumption, at the end of his first year at Darlington. It was a holiday, of course. Soon after breakfast the boys all gathered at the duckpond. The heat of the August morning lay like a hot hand on the woods and the fields.

The river was perfect for swimming these days, refuge and relaxation in the thundery weather. "Today gives you your great chance," Denny Whalen told John. "If you can swim across the duckpond, you're made."

"Yes, and if I'm not made, I'm drowned."

"Baloney," Dan Curtin said. "Your pals of the sunny corner would never let you down. We'll watch you every moment. If you can't make it, I'll pull you out myself."

"That's O. K. But what does it say in the Scriptures about the blind leading the blind?"

The boys broke into laughter in which Dan joined with the rest. "O.K., sissy," he taunted.

John's jaw set in a hard line. "I'll show you." He waded into the stream, flattened out with a belly flop, and dog-paddled out into the deep water. Frank McCue and Pete Rush ran over the bridge to the other bank of the stream, waded into the water with encouragement and taunts.

Painfully John struggled through the water, puffing like a winded hippo. He lifted his head. Halfway across! Would he make it? He thrashed and paddled with increased determination. Frank and Pete stood in the shallows of the far bank. They helped John to his feet. "You made it, Weissmuller," Frank shouted. John spat out a big stream of water.

"Ya . . . yes, I made it all right," he puffed, "but I've come to the conclusion that I'm a man—not a mackerel. I'll stick to the shore with the higher primates." John held to his resolution. He loved to play in the water, but he never got far beyond the dog-paddle stage.

Whenever his swimming prowess came up for discussion John was quick to explain: "I'm using McCue's technique when it's his turn to wake us up in the morning. He always gives a terrific knock, shouts out *'Benedicamus Domino,'* one foot on the floor. That's good advice for my swimming."

In other sports John made some progress. He spent reflective hours fishing the waters of the Ramapo under the expert guidance of Father Heimbaugh, the Izaak Walton of the faculty.

He hunted the hills with a twenty-two, and he took up golf. His golf, like his swimming, was indifferent.

There was no lack of success in his classes. John stood near the top of his group in the frequent examinations. He was determined to master the complete knowledge of a priest. "It's not what's in your notes," John observed more than once, "but what's in your head."

Time seemed to eat up the well-planned days. In due course John received his minor orders, and moved into the main hall. His room was on the second floor, near the front entrance. The eternal polishing of the lovely floors sometimes irritated him. "I'd like to suggest a new minor order for this place. 'Floor Polisher,'" he said one day to the gang. They fell in with his fancy.

One of the other boys observed with a laugh, "They would give us a sheepskin. That would be the outward sign."

"Remote preparation for the purple," someone added.

"You can't polish an apple with sheep's wool," John said. "Silk is best for that."

On May 26, 1933, at the end of his third year at Darlington, John received the sub-diaconate with his class. For him this serious step called for no heart-searching. God had called him to be a celibate priest. He took the step almost gaily. Saint Paul had said in the words of the Lord, "My grace is sufficient for thee." John had worked his way through philosophy and most of theology without a hitch; he had taken minor orders. God would take care of the rest.

The sub-diaconate imposed the duty of the daily recitation of the *Divine Office*. With his studies and other duties pressing in on all sides, John found the *Office* difficult at first. Just when he planned to devote time to this great prayer of the Church one of the gang would drop in for a chat, or there would be some unexpected demand for his services. He learned to seek out a lonely corner of the grounds or the quiet of the chapel. Both provided a good background for the psalms and the lessons which the Church had saved and bound up in the book of prayers of her priests.

New tasks went went the new honor, over and above the task of the *Office*. John took his turn as sub-deacon at the solemn masses in the seminary and at the cathedral. The complicated ceremonial demanded an accurate knowledge of the rubrics and a certain mastery of the plain chant. Moving with grace in the sanctuary, singing the Epistle at the proper time, called up in John twinges of nervousness. But when at the Offertory John assumed the humeral veil and finally received the paten, he had time to fall into a contemplation of himself and his calling. While the rhythm of the Mass went upward toward its climax in the consecration and descended to the communion, there was time to reflect upon the love of God and man.

The last year at Darlington intensified and complicated the hurried character of his life. John became a deacon December 25, 1934. In this year the chief emphasis in studies was shifted from the intellectual training for the priesthood to the practical duties of the priest. Pastoral theology insisted upon a full knowledge of the daily duties of a priest, the best and most practical means of carrying the faith to the people.

Early in this important year John had been elected prefect of his class. It was an honor he didn't crave. The duties of the office bored him, not because he became in a sense the liaison officer between the faculty and the students, but rather because he did not like the eminence. He was shy of any honor which set him apart from the average student. It was his good fortune not to hold the position long. An attack of acute appendicitis sent him to the hospital. Another student was chosen in his place. John lengthened out his convalescence and managed to shift the burden of honor to the new man. Now he could be himself again. His operation had proved to be a blessing in disguise.

John was doubly busy after his enforced absence. He was now practicing his Mass in private, and trying to achieve some familiarity with the proper procedure of administering the sacraments.

The end of the last year was crammed with activity. Studies, canonical examinations, lists of friends to be invited to his ordination and first mass, and the daily grind of studies and newly-assumed duties.

Some of the new deacons had quite a dignified and pompous air, but John would have none of this. "I could never be one of the pomp-and-circumstance boys," he confessed to a close friend. "I'm too Irish, I guess. The minute my pride gets the upper hand I begin to see myself as I really am, and that's always good for a laugh. Then I take a look at my brother Francis. He's a layman and I'm to be a priest. But Francis can give me cards and spades. 'Good as gold,' they say of Francis. But gold is soft; Francis is hard like diamond. His sparkle is what he is."

In those last visits home, before ordination, John realized once more how close were the ties which knit him to his family. His father and mother were growing old, except in their love for him. All through the long period of his studies, especially in the years of depression, they had tried to keep from him all hints of financial difficulties of any kind. But he knew that his years at Darlington were built on innumerable small sacrifices heaped up before him by Dad and Mother, Anna and the boys. These sacrifices were all the more precious because those who had made them had never once considered them as sacrifices.

Until the year John went to Darlington he had always spent his summers working for the Public Service. Now, the men he had worked with clubbed together to buy him a handsome traveling bag. This and other gifts piled up in the living room at home. Surrounded by his family, John went over and over his list of guests. No one must be left out. The family suggested and amended until the list was foolproof, nearly so.

Seated on the divan with his arm about his mother, and Anna hanging on his shoulder, John helped to put the last things in order. Above all, he tried to keep the family from growing formal or distant with him—they were all very Irish, and his new dignity had a transcendant worth in their eyes.

John countered this tendency by intensifying his jokes and quips. From his first casual greeting, "It's me, Ma!" when he bounced in through the front door, until he left to return to the seminary, he put himself out to set no distance between himself and them. As of old, he helped his mother set the table and cook the meal; he laughed and shouted and sang with the others. "After all, Dad, this is an ordination, not a funeral," John reminded his father.

Beneath the blithe mask, however, John felt the serious import of the occasion. He brought a depth of new consecration to the final retreat.

On the morning of his ordination, June 15, 1935, John came out into the drive before the hall. His new cassock was spotless. Before the other members of his class came to join him, John had a last chance to look about the grounds. He had been happy at Darlington. No millionaire living in the great hall had ever felt the richness which belonged to him on this morning of farewell.

The twenty-five men in the class gathered in the big circle before the front entrance and then filed into the small bus crammed with baggage. These last days they had all been tense and excited. Many of them had not slept well; the ordination ceremony would be several hours in duration; there would be no food for any of them until it was over.

The procession to the cathedral, the litanies while he lay stretched out flat in the supplication of prayer, the hands of the bishop upon his hands, the touching of the chalice and paten, the binding of his hands with a linen cloth, all passed for John with dreamlike swiftness. His concentration was so complete that he seemed lifted above time. Yet he realized his mother and father must be weeping there in the church, tears not of sorrow, but of joy. He was "a priest forever according to the order of Melchizedek."

In the cathedral yard families awaited their priest sons. John's first blessings were for father, mother, and the family.

"The blessing of the omnipotent God: Father, Son, and Holy Spirit, descend upon you and remain with you forever." John's hands throbbed with affection as they touched his father's gray head, then his mother's, then all the children, beginning with Anna.

John's first Mass held for him the same magic quality he had experienced at ordination. St. Rose's parish had turned out in full force. The upper church, newly completed, was not big enough to hold the crowds. John caught a glimpse of those dear family faces in the front pews when he came up the aisle with his deacon, Father McCue, and his subdeacon, Father Whalen.

The blessings after the Mass seemed endless. The Sisters had

brought him a cup of coffee into the sacristy. He was grateful
for their thought. Pale he was, and almost exhausted with the
exaltation of the morning. He still had to look forward to the
formal breakfast in St. Rose's Hall. Once again John realized
how much of love he owed to all who had made these things
possible. Then there would be a reception at the house: the
family, friends, neighbors, and acquaintances. The parlor would
ring with laughter and congratulations. The social force of the
new priest began to make itself felt with his ordination.

Shortly after his solemn Mass, John and some of his classmates
drove to Atlantic City for a rest. The newly-made priests met at
the house on Twelfth Street. Mrs. Washington solemnly charged
them: "I'm worried about John. Ever since his operation last
year he has lost weight. You can see how seedy he looks."

"It's true," Father Curtin admitted. "John does look thin and
white."

"Oh, Ma!" John protested. "I'll be all right."

His mother shook a warning finger at him. "All right is too
little. You rest twelve hours every day, drink plenty of milk, and
don't stay too long in the sun. And remember, just a few rounds
of golf, if you *must* play."

"O. K., Ma!"

"Remember, I'm going to ask Father Whalen how you behaved."

The moment John got a whiff of sea air he was a changed
man. After Mass in the morning the boys took off for eighteen
holes of golf. Against all their advice, John chopped his way
about the course in his usual fashion. He sweated, sang, and
jumped about like an amiable grasshopper. In the afternoon, on
the blazing white of the sand, he played ball and tortured his
companions into wrestling matches. Then, dashing into the surf,

he rode in and out on the breakers. In two weeks he had gained almost fourteen pounds.

Back at Twelfth Street, his mother looked at her tanned and radiant son. "Ah, I told you the rest would do you good," she exulted. "You never looked better." John peered at his friends with a grimace which warned them to be silent. Once they were out in the street again the young priests roared with laughter.

"Rest, rest!" cackled Dan Curtin. "We're the ones that need the rest. I'm worn to a shadow of myself."

John's initial year in the priesthood was spent at St. Genevieve's in Elizabeth, New Jersey—a pleasant first assignment. There, wtih nervous hesitancy, he learned to apply the lessons of Theology, Liturgy, and life. Long hours in the confessional and visits to the sick and dying perfected him in the serious graces which went with his new priesthood.

If he seemed to be set above the people, he was also their servant. John learned to appreciate this from firsthand experience. Sick calls in the middle of the night; calls to the parlor of the modest gray-shingled rectory on Livingstone Street, around the corner from the pleasant church; baptisms; teaching catechism in the school—all these demanded his best. With a kind of joy John threw himself into the new life. Yet he found time for music, scouting activities, and the welcome job of coaching a baseball team. The children loved him, their parents found him stimulating and sympathetic.

John's year at St. Genevieve's was followed by another year at St. Venantius in Orange, New Jersey. Here he was nearer to home. In a few minutes a bus could take him to the end of Twelfth Street.

It was a difficult year. His father was not well at times, and the big hospital in the parish took endless hours of selfless service.

To those who were sick John's buoyant personality was a welcome relief.

Even on his free days he left his mother's telephone number at the hospital switchboard. At home with his family he would sit near the phone. He never grumbled at the demands made on him.

"I'll be right over," he always replied. With a quick kiss for his mother, he would dash off to the latest call. Free day or not, he had an extreme sense of responsibility, which he cloaked under a mask of humor or a wisecrack. "The customer is never wrong. I can't ask people to die at hours to suit *my* convenience."

Though John never grumbled he must have had a sense of relief when he was assigned to St. Stephen's in Arlington, New Jersey. There he found himself in an intense center of activity which called out the best in him.

He arrived at his new station in the midst of the cornerstone laying for the splendid new church. He made himself useful at once.

Father Murphy was one of the most beloved pastors in the diocese. He was a father to his people and doubly a father to his assistants. "Me boys," he called them. John and his friend, Father Gordon Byrne, found themselves at home in that warm atmosphere. They were consulted before events, and praised or excused after them. The pastor always expected great things of people, especially his priests, but he repaid effort with fervent congratulation, and in the warmth of his love he was first to excuse well-intentioned failure.

A large school, ably run by the Sisters of Charity, stole a great deal of time from the two young priests. Clubs, instructions, sports, and plays—there was always something in the making.

Father Murphy set the pace, but he was careful to see that his men had days for themselves.

"All work and no play—that's an old saw," he would observe, "but it's true."

Perhaps John's best friends in the parish were the Schroths. Dr. Schroth was an exceptional man. The year after he finished his course in dentistry at Georgetown he hung out his shingle in Arlington. Almost at once misforune pounced upon his future; he was struck down with a progressive curvature of the spine. For months he lay helpless in the hospital, no once expecting him to live. Slowly, painfully he pulled himself from the lip of the grave. Never again would he practice. His wife, Josephine, returned to her job in the public schools.

People who might have expected the Schroth home to be gloomy would have been disappointed. Dr. Schroth's days were radiant with laughter. He learned to read intensively, and thus kept his mind supple and lively. In the evening, with Josephine at the piano, the Schroth home was like a little lighthouse.

Neighbors dropped in for amiable discussions or games. When he was free, John would dash in for a moment to join the group listening to a Rudy Vallee program.

He would tease his hosts unmercifully, and he made clownish faces at them when they gathered around the piano to sing the popular "Girl of My Dreams." John's soaring tenor was much admired.

Whenever Mrs. Schroth had a fit of discouragement, John sent her comical cards and drifted in and out of the house like a breeze.

"My second home," he called the Schroth household. There can be little doubt that the young priest learned a great deal from the gallant spirit, which made this home happy.

The death of his father in 1938 filled John with sorrow, and laid heavy demands upon his cheerfulness. He long remembered the sudden call home in the evening. His father was dying, that father who had seemed to him the type of everything virtuous and godlike. Hurrying through the streets, the young priest recalled his whole childhood, out of which happy frame the face of his father glowed.

John had rushed up the steps and shed his coat in the parlor. His mother and the children were in the bedroom. The prayers for the dying had begun.

"Dad!"

With a great effort his father put out one cold hand for a moment. A smile called the old beauty back to his ravaged face.

"Now John is here, everything will be all right."

John remembered these last words after the funeral. They were like a bugle call to him. Whenever he was tempted to let his temper go, or let discouragement swamp him, they called him back to balance. And if he remembered his father's tenderness and goodness now with a great sense of loss, what must his mother feel? But he could do something about that.

He dropped in at all sorts of odd hours. On his free days, and sometimes on Sunday afternoons, he was with his mother. He took her to shows and restaurants, bought her flowers and gifts, and always introduced her as "My girl."

On a Sunday in December, 1941, John took his mother to a movie and an early supper. On the way home in the car he snapped on the radio. Mrs. Washington and John sat in silence in the moving car, while all the details of the fire and death at Pearl Harbor emerged.

Looking up at her son, Mrs. Washington saw tears on his cheeks. She put one hand on his arm.

At home John kissed his mother. "Sorry I've got to run. I'm on duty at the house tonight. He turned at the door. "Of course you know I must try to enlist. Everyone will be needed." For once he had no jaunty further word.

Father Murphy was in full accord with John's determination and assisted his curate in every way. First John tried the navy. He could not pass the physical test because of the condition of his eyes.

It was a blow to the young priest. "Try the Army," Father Murphy advised. "You'll get in, I'm sure. That's where I was in World War I, and it's not such a bad outfit. Not classy like the Navy, but when the chips are down, who's looking for class?"

Rejection by the Navy doctors had shaken John's confidence. All his life he had hated the glasses he was forced to wear. He took Father Murphy's advice and applied for an Army post. The move was made with little hope. He haunted the mailbox, offered Masses, and prayed that the response might be affirmative. How could he ever think of himself again as a regular guy if they rejected him for good?

To John's intense delight the Army took him. It was hard leaving his mother, doubly hard, because Leo and Francis were enlisting. John found, however, that his mother could be gallant too. She deplored her own tears which she couldn't hold back, but she said: "I'm proud of my boys. The country needs you, and I'm glad to see you doing the right thing."

John was sent to Fort Benjamin Harrison for his preliminary training. Leo went to the Army; Francis, to the Officers' Training School for the Air Corps.

John was glad to take his training in the Middle West. The open Indiana prairie delighted him. He threw himself into the rough life of the camp. Sometimes, watching the men, he was sorry he could not join them in the actual physical struggle against the enemy. They can take it, and so can I, he thought.

On his first furlough, John caught a flight to Newark. His brothers happened to be home and decided to play a trick on him. In letters to Francis, John had complained: "The only pain in the neck is that saluting business. When I go to town I always turn my back and look in the store windows whenever I see a gang of soldiers coming by."

On the night of John's return, Francis and Leo stationed themselves on the walk a short distance above their home. In the falling dusk John's taxi drove up before the house. The two boys sauntered slowly toward the house. At the moment John turned from paying the taxi driver, the two men froze in a snappy salute. John dropped the cigarette he was smoking and returned the salute. They could hear him muttering to himself. Then he stalked by them and went across the yard. The two men whistled at the retreating back. John whirled. Recognition flooded him. In a moment all three, their arms linked, were hooting with laughter.

John paid them back later that first evening. The two boys were in a hot argument over the rival excellence of the Army and the Air Force. John was deep in conversation with Anna and his mother. Suddenly he jumped to his feet and towered above his brothers.

"Less noise!" he cried in a tough voice. "I'm still boss here. And if you don't like it, come out in the yard and put on the gloves." It was his old challenge.

"Yes, Lieutenant," they replied with mock meekness. In a moment they were all scuffling with one another.

John's overseas posting came soon after he had completed his training course. On his last furlough he was plagued with an attack of hives. His mother would have kept him at home, but John demurred. "I admit I feel sleazy," he told his mother, "but I've simply got to see everyone. I'm not going off on any boat without seeing my old pals. Not with my dog paddle. Just to be on the safe side I've got to see the nuns and everyone possible. I'm going to need all the prayers I can get."

Father Whalen was in the hospital at the time. John rushed over for a visit with his friend of long standing. He was a fountain of wit and good cheer. Father Whalen would never have guessed that John had not been well. Standing in the doorway, in the moment of departure, John was serious.

"I feel funny about this whole business," he confessed. "You won't forget me, Din?" Then he was gone.

On the last morning of his leave, John said Mass for his mother, family, and friends.

"Good by, Ma," he said at least. "No cryin'. You'll be hearing from me."

From where the four chaplains stood at the lee rail there was nothing to be seen except the ships of the convoy and their escorts, heading into the wind but bucking a current that seemed to be sliding southward off the shelf of Labrador.

On their last visit to the chart room Captain Greenspun had

shown them exactly where they were, making a little dot on the map with the help of dividers and parallel rules.

An inch or so away—on the chart—the coast of Greenland seemed to be extending her peninsulate fingers in greetings, urging the little convoy on to safe haven.

After that everyone felt better for a day or so. Then word was bruited about that both Captain Greenspun and Lieutenant Arpaia had a feeling they were being followed by enemy submarines. They couldn't explain it. It was just their psychological radar.

Lookouts were doubled, and the man in the crow's nest was relieved every hour so that his eyes wouldn't be tired or his faculties dulled by the numbing cold. A rough assignment it was, lookout on the ship's main deck. High above the bridge and deck a little roost no cozier than a barrel was fastened to the mast and in it the lookout stood, straining his eyes for signs of a snorkel tube, a torpedo's wake, or any other hostile movement. The rim of the crow's nest hit him at the armpits. His face was lashed by the wind and sleet and snow.

When the boat rolled, which was most of the time, the main mast swung back and forth like a great inverted pendulum, and the sailor in the crow's nest felt like a pea in a bucket that some small boy was swinging around his head.

The chaplains could sense that the men were worried. They knew that every man aboard the *Dorchester* had a mysterious feeling that the ship was in critical danger.

The month of January was torn off the calendar in the main mess, and the act made the trip seem interminable. The men thought they had been at sea two months now and began to doubt whether the skipper and the navigator knew where they were. At night, when most of the lights had been extinguished, there was the sound of sobbing from some of the youngsters who had never been away from home before and who, overnight, were expected to be grown men. It was a funny thing that even the toughest of the old timers never mentioned the nocturnal weeping. Even the four sky pilots had no cure for such heartache.

On the evening of the second day of the new month one of the three Coast Guard cutters blinked a message across the water to the troopship.

We are being followed by a submarine.

Captain Greenspun alerted his officers. The PA system crackled with orders and the gun crews jumped to their guns. In the engine room, in response to the telegraph from the bridge, the *Dorchester's* machinery whined and labored, but the best it could do was to push the ungainly freighter along at ten knots.

Ten knots is incredibly slow. A man can run as fast for a short while. If you subtract the distance lost by constant zig-zagging it is easy to see how helpless the *Dorchester* was, wallowing along in the winter seas.

The old man, pacing up and down the bridge, silent, troubled, deeply concerned for the safety of all the lives in his care, never seemed to rest. He had slept no more than three hours in midday since leaving port, and the quartermaster had to keep hot coffee going to the bridge in a steady stream to prevent the skipper from falling asleep.

Out of the overcast the next day came a slow, lumbering patrol plane bearing Canadian insignia on the undersides of her wings. She looked frail and antique, but none the less "Sparks" flashed her a message by blinker, giving the *Dorchester's* position and asking for assistance. Back came the stuttering light flashes:

Planes on duty elsewhere. Impossible to send any at this time.

That night the soldiers were sure that fate had kicked them squarely in the seat of the pants. They felt sorry for themselves and cursed the rust-bucket the government had given them for a transport. They wrote letters home in a blind rebellion against their miserable lot, against the bitter winds and the raw cold that made every minute on deck a trial. Many a letter was blurred by tears that wouldn't stay back.

Men ate in subdued anger and fear. They fell into the chow lines with their life jackets on, the strings securely fastened, and no one thought it strange or cowardly.

After the evening meal the tables were moved and the equipment cleared away, and the GIs had a party. Mess boys from Cuba and Puerto Rico brought out instruments. An old upright piano that had been lashed to a bulkhead was freed of its fetters, moved into the mess hall, secured again and made to give forth music. There were hot rumbas and hotter jazz and, best of all, the old familiar, popular songs that any American kid over eight knows how to sing.

The four chaplains led the singing. When the lads were a little slow on suggesting the next tune, Fox or Goode or one of the others would slip in a request for a hymn. They seemed a little out of place sandwiched in between "Mademoiselle from Armentières" and "Everything's Up To Date in Kansas City," but the troops never let the chaplains down. They sang the hymns as lustily as they did the pop tunes.

Anyone who wanted to could have looked around at the scene and pierced through the false sense of jollity. Along the bulkheads and in the corners huddled many of the men, their faces reflecting no happiness from the singing, their hearts crying out within them for surcease from suspense, for an even break with the weather and for an end to the terror that stalked through the depths of the sea.

Many a man sat with a hand plunged deep in a pocket, fingering the beads of a rosary or touching the familiar celluloid that protected a photograph of mother, wife or sweetheart. Men who have ridden out storms in damaged airplanes or suffered long hours at sea, buffeted by gales and mountainous waves, know the strange power such a talisman can give.

They must have worked their wonders that night of February 2. Although it seemed that every man could fairly taste submarines in the seething water behind them, the *Dorchester* ploughed on and the next day gained shelter behind the boom at St. John's, Newfoundland.

The sun came out and while the freighter was tied up to the pier, safe from all danger, the GIs shouted at the few girls who wandered down to the docks, sang happily and acted as if they had won the war already.

The chaplains, with special passes, went ashore to mail the letters written by the troops too late to go off in the regular pouches. In the Bachelor Officers' Quarters they shot the breeze with American officers from the Argentia base, with Canadian pilots and with the skippers of the little Canadian corvettes with which the Dominion was battling bravely against the hordes of under sea craft that Admiral Doenitz and Hitler thought could win the war war by strangulation.

They'd have been better off—in a way—if they'd stayed on board the *Dorchester*.

The news was bad. At sea, with little to go on, the four chaplains had guessed how bad it was. On shore, where men were closer to day-to-day operations, the picture in all its somber colors unfolded—threatening, bleak, blood-curdling.

To the four chaplains the word was passed that sinkings were averaging as high as a hundred a month. The landings in North Africa, the top priority convoys to Montgomery in Tripoli, the big UK runs from New York to Liverpool—all these were extending the Allied sea power too thin. Subs, fitted with their snorkel tubes, able to remain submerged with only a device the size of a mackerel above the surface, were raiding convoys and cutting out the prize targets like cowboys roping fat heifers from a moving herd.

"The Murmansk run is pure poison," the chaplains were told. "Almost no one comes back from that. It's a little better on the runs to England but those ships are faster. That rust bucket of yours can't be any bargain. Must be mighty slow."

Slow? Lord in Heaven, that she was, and the sky pilots knew it and had to go on acting as if it were the *Queen Elizabeth* or the *Wakefield*. There was nothing for them to do but put on an act and try to kid the soldiers along, and whenever there was any spare time or when they were getting the little bit of horizontal drill they needed each night they could pray to God for a safe landing in Greenland.

There isn't much else to do with an elephantine 5000 ton freighter whose engines couldn't turn up another knot if they were fed aviation gas.

The respite in port was too short to do anyone much good.

A little after the church bells of St. John's had marked eight o'clock in the evening the *Dorchester* quit the pier and passed out to sea, through the submarine boom at the harbor mouth.

The convoy moved on northeastwards, through the strange white darkness of an Arctic night. Each ship, it seemed to the men at the *Dorchester's* rail, stuck up like a clay target in a shooting gallery, inviting a torpedo from any sub that was within miles of the wallowing convoy.

On deck the crew made last minute moves to secure odd gear and to lash the canvas covers on the hatches. In the brittle silence of the northern night each sound seemed maddeningly loud, each noise a gilt edged invitation to a sub commander.

In and out of the compartments below decks the four chaplains moved unceasingly, trying to visit every man before he sacked out for the night. They joked and kidded them and did the things they had to do, not knowing whether everything was futile or not. Being Men of God, they would have done it anyway, sure that they themselves should never essay the passing of judgment, yet because they were also smart, normal men, they had their moments of doubt. What counted most was that they kept their doubts to themselves. The men saw in them the faith they wished they had themselves and never wondered if what they saw was real.

Their influence was felt by everyone aboard the *Dorchester*. Each brave smile, each kind word set off its own chain reaction. But so too did other moods. Once when a soldier, late in the evening, visited the chaplains' cabin to borrow a Bible, he stumbled out of the companionway and into the room to find Washington, the young Catholic priest, and Goode, the young Jewish Rabbi, talking in muted tones, solemn-faced and deep in conference.

Bible in hand, the GI scurried back below decks, and the story raced the rounds that the padres were desperately worried about the chances of making Greenland before the Nazis learned of the slow convoy's whereabouts.

They *were* afraid. Visions of submarines slinking along in the black depths, altering their course to match the altered courses of the freighter, came naturally before them. They were afraid, yes, but they were not cowards.

In the middle of the night some of the soldiers sleeping in the compartments farthest below decks heard the engine room telegraph bells jingle and after that the *Dorchester* moved through the water more slowly. Up on the bridge Captain Greenspun had ordered speed reduced because he was running into pan ice, and knew that at any minute an iceberg might loom ahead out of the harmless slush.

From here on into port in Greenland engines would run at half speed, the propeller blades would turn even more slowly because of the new threat.

Strangely the slower speed brought a sense of relief, both on the bridge and among the men bunking in the holds. The old man, knowing that the knife sharp edges of an iceberg could rip a U-boat as a can opener splits open a tin of sardines, figured no submarine would operate in such dangerous waters.

The chaplains congratulated each other. They knew about the ice and its double portent—of danger and of safety both—and they knew that probably by now the convoy had moved far enough to the north to come under the protecting umbrella of patrol planes flying off Greenland's runways.

The weather grew nastier with each passing hour. Long ground swells battered the stumbling *Dorchester,* and in between white-capped waves hammered malignantly against her bows and shook her to her keel plates.

Winds whetted to knife-like sharpness on the icefields of the polar cap clawed at the ship and the men who had to be above decks. The marrow-chilling cold found its way beneath whatever clothing a man could wear. On the bridge, in the crow's nest and in the gun tubs men wore felt face masks. Their breath congealed about the lower half of the masks and a rime of ice covered their collars.

The Arctic night was beautiful but it was deadly. Like a toy being dragged by a loitering child the *Dorchester* made her way through the early hours of the darkness—a darkness overcast with an eerie glimmering of whiteness. It zigged and zagged and it seemed to stumble from one crest to another, being punished by each in turn, yet staggering slowly on.

Below decks the passage of time was a slow gnawing at the mind, a dull sawing on the raw and open nerve ends of the soul.

There seemed to be an apprehensive silence that brooded over the ship. Men in their bunks sensed it, their eyes wide and their muscles tense. With the cutting of the speed the screws no longer threshed half the time out of water. The silence of the Arctic night muffled the clank of the engines.

The ship's bells struck twice. It was one o'clock in the morning. They never sounded again.

A minute or so later a torpedo smashed into the *Dorchester,* well below the water line amidships.

The stricken ship staggered from the explosion. Men lying fully clothed in their bunks were tossed to the decks like walnuts from an upset basket. Others were catapulted against the bulkheads.

Blackout lights went out instantly, plunging the entire ship into darkness and leaving the men to grope in terror as they fought their way topside.

The German submarine skipper had caught the freighter fair on his periscope's crossed hairs. The torpedo, running swift and true, ripped open the tender skin of the ship and exploded in all its fury in the engine room.

Steam lines burst letting their vapor escape to kill and scald and torture the engineers and oilers. Fuel tanks split open, spewing their oily contents over the scene of terror, making each ladder and catwalk a place of peril.

A wiper, checking the bearings in the shaft alley, heard the explosion, felt the ship tremble and died in a sudden tidal wave of water and oil.

A junior engineer, standing at the side of a boiler, was flung against the water jacket unconscious, and awoke to die in a searing, blinding burst of steam.

In thirty seconds a hundred men were dead, scalded, mutilated or drowned like rats in a trap.

Soldiers scrambled toward the companionways, already leaning crazily as the *Dorchester* listed to port, and fought their way, cursing and screaming, to the windy deck.

Abandon-ship drills, lectures on survival in torpedoings and the military discipline so newly acquired by civilians-suddenly-turned-soldiers went by the boards. In each man's mind was the single thought of how to save himself. The mores and the teachings of civilization were cast aside as a snake sheds its skin in the spring.

Then out of chaos came brief signs of order as men conquered the fear that had shortcircuited their thinking. Doctors and medics snatched up their kits and headed below, bucking the tide of men seeking the open decks. If they sensed their own danger they brushed it aside and went on to rescue the injured. Their flashlights stabbed feebly at the blackness of the holds, already reeking with the choking fumes of ammonia.

Far below them in the engine room a boiler blew up, mangling bodies already mangled by the torpedo's warhead.

Up above things were no better. Even before the *Dorchester* had recovered from the first shock the skipper clawed for the siren lanyard to send off the six blast signal agreed upon before the convoy quit home waters.

Three times the siren roared. The fourth blast died in the whistle's metal throat, a hollow, mocking cough.

Because of the freighter's list, lifeboats on the starboard side hung inboard, and men struggled to free them. Some were lowered, bumping crazily down the ship's sloping sides. Others broke away and fell free, hurtling down upon men who had jumped overboard in the first seconds of terror.

The wind meanwhile had chopped around to the northwest and some of the lifeboats, safely launched, were breached by heavy seas which filled them to the thwarts. Men on the troopship saw them disappear, spewing soldiers into the water. Everywhere there were the red lights of the life jackets, twinkling on the water like sparks of fire.

Life rafts went over the side as frantic men hacked at their lashings. Some bobbled away in the darkness before anyone could reach them. Others were so crowded with survivors that men died struggling to get a grip on their handlines.

Here and there about the deck battle lanterns flickered fitfully, doing little to pierce the blackness of the night.

Men shouted and men wept. Soldiers made their way out of the hold without their lifejackets and went back to get them, dying in the smothering holds.

The devout cried to God for help, while others cursed His name. Kids who should have been in bed back home, resting for a day in the fields or at football practice, called for their mothers. Some just huddled at the rail, already awash, like frightened sheep.

Hysteria compelled weak men to jump into the Atlantic with

mad words upon their lips, but the bitter cold of the ocean stilled their cries as if the words thickened in their throats.

Through this scene of terror moved a few strong men, purposeful, calm and seemingly unafraid.

A soldier who couldn't have been out of his teens cut away a rope that had tangled in the block of a davit, setting a lifeboat, crowded with men, free upon the surface of the sea.

Captain Greenspun was everywhere, encouraging the soldiers, helping the crew to launch anything that would float and issuing the few commands there were left to issue on a floundering, mortally wounded ship.

Army surgeons and medics behaved as though participating in a briefing session on how to care for the wounded at sea. Injured men were brought topside, bandaged and helped into lifeboats when these were available. Men who might have died lived because of their ministration.

And everywhere about the ship, in the terror-ridden interior and on the crazily tilted deck, the four chaplains moved among the men with helpful words, giving some the strength to live and some the courage to die.

Knowing that the life expectancy of a man in such frigid waters was somewhere between 18 and 40 minutes, the three men with Crosses on their collars and the one with the Tablets of the Law on his, urged the soldiers to stay aboard as long as possible after the smallboats had been cast off.

"Take it easy, soldier. It will be all right."

Strange how such simple, meaningless words could still panic in a man's heart. Stranger still how they could inject starch into a coward's spine.

The *Dorchester* by now had lost all way and was lying dead

in the water. Fitful winds plucked spume from the wave crests and whipped it into the faces of the men on deck.

Suddenly the ship shivered and men everywhere cried out.

"She's going down. She's going down. We'll be sucked under."

Even the GIs who had never seen the ocean until they embarked on the *Dorchester* knew the added danger that accompanies a ship's last plunge.

Like old wives' tales feeding on themselves, lurid stories of the swirling, sucking vortex created when a vessel went down had gone the rounds among the men. What had made it worse was the knowledge that the evil couldn't be exaggerated.

Now, in the blackness of the night, the terror was multiplied a thousandfold.

The chaplains sensed the threat.

"Over the side, men, make it fast." The wind tore the words from their lips.

"Swim to the lifeboats," they cried. "Get away from the ship."

Men looked at the four chaplains with new wonder. They saw them move together as though that way they could be of greater help.

Soldiers lifted their eyes to them as if for a sign, some symbol to carry with them into the valley of death.

A man—more boy than man—made his way to the group at the rail.

"Padre, I've lost my life jacket. I can't swim. I'll . . ."

One of the chaplains tore off his own and put it about the boy's shoulders.

"Take this. I'm staying. I won't need it."

The soldier tied the jacket's strings, mounted the rail and slipped into the sea, now almost level with the deck.

Of the three hundred or so men who survived not one can

remember which chaplain it was who first voiced the decision to stay with the ship.

Was it Father Washington, who couldn't swim across a duck pond? Was it Fox, survivor of one war and victim of another? Poling, heir to a great name in preaching, or Goode, the Rabbi from the Pennsylvania Dutch country?

What does it matter now? If the first had not spoken, another would. Catholic, Jew and Protestant; each proved that night that courage knows no distinction of creed, bravery no division of caste.

Violent squalls confused the dying moments of the freighter. Flares on the bridge revealed the deck, now awash, at an ugly slant. Men fought for places on the last raft, and the losers cursed and wept.

The four chaplains stood with arms linked, each one without a life jacket. Somewhere off in the seething seas four other men were cheating death, supported by the chaplains' gifts.

Icy waters reached their knees as their lips moved in prayer.

"Our Father which art in Heaven, Hallowed be Thy name. Thy kingdom come, Thy will be done . . ."

The troopship labored to rise from a trough and staggered on. Water sluiced along the sloping deck.

". . . ego te absolvo a peccatis tuis, in nomine Patris, et Filii, et Spiritus Sancti . . ."

A soldier, bleeding through his bandages, crawled to where the four were standing. His voice was barely audible.

"God bless you," he said, and crawled into the sea.

A wave breached clear across the tilted deck.

"Hear, O Israel, the Lord Our God, the Lord is one . . ."

For an instant the light of a flare cast an effulgence upon the four of them for all who were left aboard to see.

". . . forgive us our trespasses, as we forgive those who trespass against us . . ."

Once more the ship labored to breast the next wave. There was a great noise of water and air churning in the darkness.

The *Dorchester* fought to right herself, failed, and plunged beneath the surface.